M000074836

SIGNS AND WONDERS

SOJOURN IN THE INNER-CITY

Angela Punky Stultz

Copyright © by Angela Punky Stultz

All rights reserved. Without limiting the rights under copyrights reserved above, no part of this publication may be reproduced, stored in a retrieval system or transmitted , in any form or by any means without the prior written permission of the author and publisher, or in the case of photocopying or other reprographic copying. All rights reserved. No part of this publication may be reproduced, distributed, or transmitted in any form or by any means, including photocopying, recording, or other electronic or mechanical methods, without the prior written permission of the publisher, except in the case of brief quotations embodied in critical reviews and certain other noncommercial uses permitted by copyright law. For permission requests, write to the publisher, addressed "Attention: Permissions Coordinator," at the address below.

This publication contains the opinion, ideas and experience of the author and is designed to provide useful advise on the subject matter covered. There are lessons to be learned and as such can be replicated. At the same time this publication is not intended to provide a basis for action without consideration and involvement of professionals. The author and publisher expressly disclaim any responsibility for any liability, risk, personal or otherwise, which is incurred as a consequence directly or indirectly of the use and application of any of the contents of this book.

Published by Kindle Direct Publishing
Second Edition
22 21 20 19 4 3 2

ISBN 978-1-08000-738-7
1. Social work, 2.Community, classes, races
3. Poor in cities. Slums, 4. Youth, adolescents empowerment
5. Gender equality, 6. Non government organizations (NGO's)

Photograph of zinc fence: Tiumion Bowers
Photograph of Jamaican villa: Marilyn Winkworth
Author's photograph: Rob Niezen
Book design and cover: Rob Niezen

Visit: https://angelastultz08.wixsite.com/pasbooks

SIGNS AND WONDERS

SOJOURN IN THE INNER-CITY

Stories of Triumph and Trials in
Community Development & Peace Building

Praise for Signs and Wonders

Signs and Wonders: Sojourn in the Inner-City is a fresh account of Jamaican ghetto life. It is absolutely authentic. As a close-up observer of much of Angela's Journey, I can testify to that. You have only to open the book and you too will see it.
Horace Levy, civil rights activist

Written with powerful insight into life in an impoverished community in Kingston Jamaica. and into the culture of youth gangs and the anxious mothers. The stories are powerful yet beautifully textured with breathtaking moments. In one story Angela describes the discrimination she experience as a Rastafarian woman. A complex and vividly-written piece. This book is a must-read!
Joyce Mackenzie, Chair Board of Directors Jamaican Self-Help

This is a fine and faithful account of one woman's remarkable courage, tenacity and compassion in managing for many years a community project in West Kingston, Jamaica. It changed the lives of many hundreds of the most marginalized people with schooling, employment training, counselling, basic health care and peace building.
Angela Stultz is a heroine of mine, and a valued partner of Jamaican Self-Help Canada.
She has had the additional gift of absorbing Canadian volunteers in the work, to provide them with meaningful cross cultural experience. Her story, so honestly and modestly told , is a model for all international development efforts. But it is primarily a testament to Jamaican goodness and ingenuity through many challenging years. I hope "Signs and Wonders", an

inspirational work, will be read by many, north and south.
Rosemary Ganley, author and co-founder of Jamaican Self-Help

In this beautiful publication, Signs and Wonders: Sojourn in the Inner-City, we have the rare opportunity of having this story told by Angela Stultz who has been on the ground and in the gutter doing the actual work, walking the actual walk, talking the actually talk. It therefore is so refreshing, so engaging and so authentic a voice that reading it rivets you to page after page, story after story.

What we have is a first-hand, upfront opportunity to see humanity at its most vulnerable and in its different shapes and forms, to hear about discrimination and abuse and to celebrate in a way that sometimes is bittersweet. Most importantly, we learn that with the right ingredients and invested partners, we can come up with and effect solutions for change. A precedent has been set, the bar has been raised by and for us. Another generation therefore has no excuses.

If I am to sum it all up, we learn that sparkling diamonds abound in our communities and when treated with respect and dignity, will shine to worldwide proportions. Signs and Wonders: Sojourn in the Inner-City is doing just that in now teaching this to partners around the world.

From an entirely jealous perspective those of us who know Angela personally, triumph and celebrate with her on this her milestone. We celebrate the splendid work she has done over the years to make our communities better places. Big up Angie!

Ian McKnight, civil society specialist

This book is dedicated to youth, especially those growing up in marginalized communities. You are significant, you are important, you are a big deal. Stay focused on your dreams, and your connectedness to the Most High God's presence in you, and around you, as you take charge of your destiny.
And read... read... ... read everything.

In memory of my grandparents, Albert and Agatha Gentles.

Table of Contents

Acknowledgements

The stories that follow reflect the memories and highlights of a fifteen-year journey in one of Kingston's most marginalized and toughest neighborhoods. They are a look back on my journey as Executive Director of the S-Corner Clinic and Community Development Organization—devising multifaceted interventions, endlessly writing grant proposals to keep the organization going; the personal, team and community risks and rewards and the networks and alliances that enabled some lasting impact. For all of it I give thanks to Jehovah Almighty for his omnipotent presence and guidance.

Along the way, I met some remarkable people without whom we could not have accomplished the transformations that occurred for individuals and the community. Some of these encounters were for specific reasons and seasons. Others led to long lasting relationships and continue to fulfill their divine mandate even today. These people are now part of my life's circle and with their advice, critique and guidance,

I was able to complete the writing and publishing of this book, telling the stories of how it was. Thank you, Marisa Kaczmarczyk, Rosemary Ganley, Brian Hanley, Natalie Gensac, Joyce McKenzie and Art Poston.

I want to pay tribute to and thank the people of Kingston 13. Their determination to work towards their own transformation, the hours we spent together, their sweat and tears, and willingness to share their stories and their lives have helped me to become a better person. Special thanks to the Community Based Organization (CBO) executive members, who provided indelible service as the community's advocate, mobilizers and fundraisers; Irvin Munroe, Winston Steele, Michael Whittingham, Ionia Smith, Marie Glanville, Marie Parkinson, Monica Rowe, Elizabeth Thomas and the late Marva Brown. I have used what I have learned from them to continue development work with a deeper understanding of the complexity of life in the inner city.

I also want to salute the staff I worked with from 1992 to 2000 and again 2004 to 2009. These are the people who went beyond job descriptions to give of themselves for community betterment: Carreen Jopp, Eric Brown, Leroy Barnett, Fabian Bernard, Barbara Salmon, Dian Peart, Beverly Rose, Michael Harris, Rudolph Garrick, Valin Barry Sinclair, Olive Hamilton, Delores Clarke, Patricia Mitchelle, Elsie Mason, the late Dr. Trevor (Butt) Lewis and the late Marlene Campbell (RIP my sister). I owe much to the founders of the S-Corner organization,

Dr. Wendell Abel and Janet Hunter, and to the S-Corner Board of Directors, Dr. Phillip Osei, Pastor Carlton Dennis and in particular Horace Levy, Carol Narcisse, Mutabaruka, and the late Sandra 'Sajoya' Alcott, who were instrumental in their invaluable, practical involvement as well as their advice and monitoring of our organization's impact. Special mention and thank you to our past international volunteer Brian Hanley who, bitten by the development bug, continues to work as a global change agent and provided me with feedback and vivid recollections towards my writing.

Our interventions would not have been possible without the financial and moral support of local and international partners, including the Environment Foundation of Jamaica, CHASE Fund, Youth Interactive Santa Barbara, Oxfam UK, Christian Aid and Jamaican Self-Help (JSH) Canada. Christian Aid and JSH Canada were there for the long run providing integral peacebuilding income generation programs, in advocating for positive policy change, and in strengthening our organizational capacity along the way.

I want to wholeheartedly express my gratitude to my chief editors and supporters Marisa Kaczmarczyk and Carol Narcisse who believed in me, made me feel comfortable to send them my many drafts for editing, and gave me their honest critique and encouragement; and to my mentors Horace Levy and Rosemary Ganley, for their suggestions and for guiding me in the

ACKNOWLEDGEMENTS

who upon learning I was writing my book, offered me
the space and resources to host my book launch any
time I was ready.

A big shout-out as well to my primary cheerleaders who
have relentlessly pushed and criticized me when they
felt I was not writing fast enough. Thank you, Lorna
(Skinny) Brown, Betty Fuller-Peters, Sandra Murphy,
Carol Narcisse, Christina Stonehouse, Pauline Davis,
Sheila Fairman and Donna Blackwood. To my
demanding dupes Myrna McKenzie, for me to "please
write the book", thanks for your ever-present shoulder
to cry on when some memories were too much for me.
And to my consistent pushers; John Catley, Barbara
Christen, Esther Sewell, Janet Grant and Judy Grant,
thank you.

To my extended family members who gave their
persistent encouragement, Pauline Bryan, Garcia
Campbell, Tricia Gentles, Laura Campbell, Melony
Stewart and Margaret Kelly, thank you.

Special mention and love to the design team for the
book; photographer Tiumion Bowers, my grandson
Zion Wright for visualizing my ideas for the book cover
and illustrator/designer Rob Niezen, whose voluntary
skill and time spent I could never afford. To his wife
Sandy MacFarlane for welcoming me in their home so
that we could finalize the design and formatting. Special

thanks to web page designer, my niece, Tara Trotter, and to Moya Rodney.

Much "appreci-love" to David Kelly and Errol Stewart who pooled their resources to purchase my laptop, giving me the tools to write. And write I did.

Special mention to my Pastor, Randolph Baker who accepts me as I truly am, a woman of God, and who encourages me, prays with me and for me as I carry through my work in marginalized communities and my writings. Thank you as well to Pastor Kirk and the Christ Alive Church, thank you for your prayers and words of encouragement. And the same to my Priestess sister-friend Empress Imani McFarlane.

Lastly, to my unconditional loves, my heartbeats who allowed me the undisturbed space to write even when it meant reducing their "me an' mommy" time: my four children, Lemoyah, Makeda, Omari and Jolee. And my life partner, Dennis Rowe, your love and encouragement: thank you all.

Editor's Note

The stories in this book are as often inspiring as they are heart breaking. It is an engaging read. The book is part memoir and part instruction manual for development practitioners interested in better understanding the underlying factors that give rise to the circumstances of people's lives.

Signs and Wonders: Sojourn in the Inner-City places the individual events of its stories in a wider context of systemic and structural barriers—some of which readers may not have considered previously. The stories not only describe the challenges of life in the inner-cities of Kingston, they also describe efforts and ways to better them.

Like Joyce Mckenzie, of Jamaican Self-Help Partners, one of the agencies which funded the work of the S-Corner Clinic and Community Development Organisation, you, the reader, may gain important insights for your work. Says Joyce: "Before reading the book and the story of Shine and Shun, we had no idea that the education programs we funded also needed practical resources to help bright students from disadvantaged communities assimilate in their schools, resources like proper shoes..."

As you read then, be prepared to laugh, cry, nod your head in recognition, wrestle with anger, be comforted by the stories of triumph and guided by the revelations.

Carol Narcisse, former Board Chair, S-Corner Clinic and Community Development Organization

Introduction

Signs and Wonders: Sojourn in the Inner-City takes the reader along the journey of a grassroots organization operating in one of Kingston Jamaica's poorest inner-city communities. Through recounting personal encounters, observations and direct interventions, *Signs and Wonders* captures the challenges that Non-Government Organizations (NGOs) and community development practitioners face. These include achieving community buy-in, overcoming biases, class and gender divisions, addressing people's sense of alienation, managing limited financial resources, and working with political cultures that view people's empowerment with suspicion.

This is not only a recounting of challenges however, for beyond them are the stories of hope, resilience and triumph.

The S-Corner Clinic & Community Development Organization was an NGO operating in Kingston 13. The community is characterized by older houses typical of early middle class Kingston, now overshadowed by rusty zinc fences, dilapidated buildings and weak sanitation disposal. The community's decline has not just been physical but also social with high levels of illiteracy, teenaged pregnancy, underemployment and gang violence.

The S-Corner organization initially provided programs in education, health, sanitation, and economic development to help to alleviate the complex issues of inter-generational poverty. The strategies were informed by the organization's integration into the community coupled with quantitative and qualitative research which unearthed a myriad of critical underlying factors hindering community development. In response, the organization broadened its scope of work to include projects such as sanitation infrastructure and peace building. As an escalating homicide rate became an increasing burden on our health care programs, costing lives and damaging the community's economy; the addition of peace-building programs was especially essential and helped to make it possible to achieve social and economic transformation in the community.

Signs and Wonders presents the reader with ten compelling short stories of the trials and triumphs. The stories illustrate the human impact of the ills experienced by many communities: unemployment, crime, gangs, domestic abuse, interpersonal conflicts, and parenting challenges. They also emphasize the triumphs and the resilience of the human spirit. The reasons for triumphs are varied and attributable to the determination of the residents, the multiple approaches of the NGO, the author's deepened faith and relationship with the creator, and to unexplainable occurrences: the signs and wonders.

It is hoped, that the stories will provoke academic debate and further discussions.

Taken as a whole, the book exposes systemic inequities which create and perpetuate poverty. It provides social workers and social work agencies with important insights and ideas for their work with vulnerable communities and challenges practitioners of community development and peace building to respond in ways that can lead to equity and justice.

Perhaps, above all, the stories are intended to inspire individuals living in difficult circumstances to believe that transformation is possible. Each story highlights a unique and personal experience and yet an underlying thread of community challenge and resilience is woven from one story to the next. All stories are true. The author has been given permission to tell individuals' stories and to use their names, although some names have been changed to protect individual identities.

These are the highlights of the stories that follow.

1. *Papa Who Made Me* The most frequent question asked of me is why? Why do I work in the field I

do and in inner-city communities? This story pays tribute to the man who most greatly influenced my life choices and to the resilience I witnessed and benefitted from as I grew up.

2. *That Address (1993)* There is a stigma attached to living in the inner-city. This story reveals the impact of such stigma on residents seeking jobs and other opportunities and on our organization's recruitment of qualified staff. It illustrates the power of forgiveness and individuals' capacity for behavioral change despite the odds. Finally, it points to the importance of social practitioners being unbiased and non-judgmental towards the people they serve.

3. *Woman Powah (1995)* tells the tale of one woman's resilience and determination to improve her life in the face of domestic abuse. It relates how our organization mobilized the community to support one of their own and it explores the alliances women forge and what can be achieved when women support one another.

4. *Mama Cry (1996)* highlights the challenges of single parenting in a turbulent neighborhood, and a mother's willpower to save her children from a life of crime and teenaged pregnancy. A police killing motivates our organization to

develop a peace building committee that works to reduce antagonism between gangs.

5. *They Called Him Bogle (1997)* focuses on a youth advocate whose mother's parenting style makes him the target of community taunting. It tells the story of this young Jamaican's life-changing introduction to a young American volunteer and how together they break unprecedented ground in the area of youth mentorship and education.

6. *Keisha and the Circle of Life* begins with a chance meeting between our organization's director and a past student at a local hospital. It highlights the importance of local partnerships between civil society groups, church organizations and citizens in programs that give back to communities and support youth to have access to education and skills training—services that are usually outside the reach of their financial means.

7. *Images of Righteousness (1999)* sheds light on reprisal killings in a community alienated by the state, and the subsequent process for peace. It provokes discussion of what is our image of righteousness.

8. *His Name Was Sheldon (2005)* is a story of the twin experiences of hope and despair that can characterize life in many inner-city communities

and the importance of psychological and emotional support for social work practitioners who are not exempt from the trauma that accompanies their work. They are the counsellors and the comforters, but who counsels them?

9. *Shine and Shun* is the tale of a child who was awarded a scholarship to a prestigious school and then struggles to assimilate. It exposes the inequities in society that are manifest in the educational system. The story challenges community development organizations to develop programs that go beyond academics to build children's self-worth.

10. *Freedom Festival (2006)* illustrates an innovative solution to gang conflict. It describes a process of bringing together reggae musicians, residents and members of our organization to form a Committee for Peace, and create an unprecedented pathway for bringing rival gang members together.

PAPA WHO MADE ME

Papa Who Made Me

The question most frequently asked of me is why. Why do I work in the field I do and in inner-city communities. What motivates me? My answer is simple. I believe we all have a divine purpose which we must carry out to make us truly happy, and there is often someone in our early life who helps to put us on our path. For me it was my grandfather. My grandpapa made me... well, he directed me, to my life purpose.

I grew up in a place called Standpipe, a low income community located in Liguanea, St. Andrew, on the outskirts of the area known as the Golden Triangle. In fact, our community is surrounded by upper middle class neighborhoods—Beverly Hills, Hope Pastures, Mona Heights and such. The women in our community were the maids and nannies to the families of these neighborhoods while the men were chauffeurs, gardeners and plumbers. Our community also provided services of mechanics, bicycle shops (one of which my papa owned), seamstresses, hairdressers, shop keepers and construction workers. Everyone worked. Whoever was not employed had their own businesses.

Poor is relative and so is rich. I grew up in a poor neighborhood thinking I was rich. My grandfather had been a construction worker in Panama, arriving there after the Panama Canal was built. The Panama Canal was a long-term USA project developed to ship commercial goods quickly and cheaply between the Atlantic and Pacific oceans. History has documented thousands of Caribbean migrants who died from the harsh, slave-like conditions they suffered while building the canal. Many migrants like my grandfather went to work as construction workers for the British and American business settlers who arrived after the canal was built. He returned home with a little nest egg. My family was one of three families who were landowners, owning large acres of land that started at the top of the lane, continued over the bridge and up to the National Chest Hospital. Our family name was known throughout the community, the "Gentles". We were one of five families with a car, and we had a Kerosene oil stove which were both symbols of relative wealth. Other community members used charcoal stoves and those even poorer used wood fire.

My grandfather spoke fluent Spanish and believed himself to be an educated man. He also believed he could have expanded his businesses—bicycle shop, grocery shop and animal farming—if only the banks had been willing to loan him the money he needed. On many occasions we would hear my grandfather swearing bitterly against the banks. He would say to mama, "Gatha, dem tun me dong and ge de chiney man an de Syrian man loan, people weh no come from Jamaaica". His swearing would be louder on weekends when he got drunk.

Being an ambitious man and determined to succeed, papa used the title to his land to borrow high interest loans from established solicitors, who incidentally were also the country's monopoly distributors of beer. As early as I can remember, my grandfather would place my outstretched hand beside his, then he would say, "my Punky, u see dis color here u have, u get no break, dem will shit on you, so me waant u to read. Read so u can become docta, and a waant yu to juck dem hard wid de needle when dem come to u hospital, sickness is not only fe de black man, sickness is fe everybaddy".

I became aware of and would also experience colorism and racism even though at the time I did not know the terms. One of the chores we had to do as children was deliver freshly picked seasonal fruits of ackee, naseberry and mangoes to the families in the affluent communities of Mona Heights and Hope Pastures and to the nearby North side Plaza. My cousins were of caramel brown complexion and one of them had a light yellow skin tone due to her Chinese mixture. Her father was the son of one of the Chinese merchants who owned the Supermarket. So she also had the "good hair" which my grandmother would brush and plait in two with the plaits hanging down her back. Although my grandmother dressed us in the identical dresses our parents had sent us from England, strangers and family members never ever paid me the attention they would shower on her. Everyone treated her like a princess, giving her unsolicited gifts and telling her how pretty she was. The families we delivered fruits to went a step further. Some of them would invite my cousin inside their home and politely ask me to wait outside on the veranda. My cousin would later emerge, her pockets filled with crumbled cakes and cookies they had given her and she had hidden for me. I loved her to death.

Colorism was also played out in the schools by the teachers themselves. Lighter complexioned and mixed race children were the teachers' pets and were elevated to class monitors and prefects. The student population referred to the teachers' pets as "pretty dunce" but why pretty? Their peers, the underachieving dark skin ones were simply "dunce bats". I remember being in third grade in Miss Jerron's class. On her desk was a big bright red truck and a white doll with blue eyes, along with miniature versions of both. These were motivational rewards for the students, male and female, with the highest grade average. At the end of the term, I received the small doll, yet I was the female student with the highest grade. My runner up was a girl of mixed race. She received the larger doll. I felt hurt and told my grandmother. I never played with dolls and had no interest in the doll, but what mattered was that I was cheated out of a prize I had worked hard for because of my complexion. The following day my grandmother showed up at the school. She was dressed in her Sunday best and questioned the teacher about her action. The teacher apologized, it was a mix-up, she said and could she get me another doll deserving of my grades? Two days later I received my doll which I immediately handed over to my cousin.

Being subjected to racism, colourism and classism all their lives, my grandparents and many other families in our community understood and promoted the value of education. My grandfather would bring home books for me and the newspaper for himself. He loved to read, especially about politics, to show off his worldly knowledge and to prepare himself for the arguments he would have in the bars with his drunken friends come weekends. The Matildas Corner bar was one of his favorite places. It sat between the Indian Barber shop and St. Peter & Paul Roman Catholic Church.

Papa took me everywhere with him. We would go to the parish library, to the bars, and to the shops as I was his assistant in our Bicycle repair business. And everywhere we went all I needed was the book I was currently reading. By the time I was nine, I had almost completed the entire Nancy Drew book series, the Hardy Boys and the Sydney Sheldon series.

To ensure I had enough books to read, I joined the Tom Redcam Library. I would take my three male friends, Miguel-Michael Stewart, Wings-David Kelly and Coolie

Tony-Anthony Green, to the library with me. We were avid readers and before the two weeks were up, we would already have exchanged the borrowed Library books within our group and excitedly discussed the stories we read. We had formed what I now know to be a book club. In addition to encouraging my love of books, Papa also taught me how to "wheelie", that is, ride a bicycle on the back wheel only while raising the front wheel high above the ground. I could play marbles, football and I was famous for climbing the highest of trees.

My grandmother would remind him I was a girl and should be playing dolls with my five female cousins. She was also concerned that I was not learning the traditional, female household chores. I never cleaned house, washed dishes, washed socks and panties like all the other little girls in the household and neighborhood. Papa ignored her, as he passed me another bicycle tyre to patch. I would run behind him if she attempted to take me to where the little girls were playing. Finally, she gave up. I knew the exact Christmas my grandmother gave up. That Christmas my cousins Neicey, Sally, Marlene, Pauline and Brenda got the prettiest dolls ever and I got a box of the shiniest marbles ever, the same as Bibs my male cousin.

My grandmother was a good Christian woman, and would wake my six cousins and I every Saturday morning at 5:30 am. At 5:45 Oral Roberts, an American evangelist preacher, would be broadcast on radio and mama would place our hands on the radio while we listened to Oral Roberts' sermon. My grandmother was illiterate and so from the age seven, as the brightest of the lot, I was given the task of reading the bible aloud, keeping up with Oral Roberts in finding every verse, chapter and Psalm he demanded we find. And then on Sunday mornings it would be church time, time to worship at St Peter and Paul Catholic Church. I didn't attend as regularly as my other cousins. My grandmother would be frustrated at my don't care attitude in getting dressed, and would go with my other cousins and leave me at the urging and promise of my grandfather. I mastered delay tactics. I was never able to find one foot of my good Sunday shoes, the ribbon worn last week that I was sure I had put in my drawer, or any of the socks she had told me to wash. My grandfather would say, "Gatha, leave har, me and mi Punky will be ready for mass latahl". Church services were held at 9 am and 11 o' clock. True to his words, by 10:30 am we were both dressed and ready. And whenever we went, immediately after church we had another equally important destination.

We spent many Sunday evenings in the bar. Papa and his friends always with their flask of Wray and Nephew overproof white rum before them, while I sat perched on the high bar stool beside him in the corner. In front of me he would place my book and a large Pepsi bottle, my drink. He assured himself I was reading and was not listening to the discussions, which sometimes induced curse words not appropriate for a child's ears. His mantra was, "Mi Punky, when you grow up you are not going to wash nobody clothes, you are going to be a Doctah, and have a maid to do those things, so you have to read, ok? Read fe papa." He would then kiss me on my forehead. Unknown to Papa I never read in the bar except when asked. I loved listening to him and his drunken friends' discussions. They discussed current issues, politics, the economy, the church, racism, colorism and classism. With a drunken slur they would ask rhetorical questions, "how comes the white people, the yellow complexion people dem sit on one side of the church and the dark skin black folks sit on the other side of the pew. Why de separation, de colar divide? Don't they serve the same Jesus?"

The discussion would switch from religion to politics and who better represented the poor now that we had gained independence from our colonial masters: Bustamante or Norman Manley? Their voices would get louder as they discussed the differences between the Bustamante Industrial Trade Union and the National Workers Union (BITU and NWU) both with strong allegiance to the respective political parties, the Jamaica Labour Party and the Peoples National Party. The loud voices would be accompanied with finger waving and pointing at each other's faces and questions would be punctuated with profanities. Sometimes, Papa would caution his friends to refrain or reduce the frequency of expletives as I was there, nevertheless he too would join in. Fighting the alcohol which now affected his speech, he would turn to me with all the soberness he could muster, asking me to promise him I would never use the words I heard in the bar. I would somberly nod my head. I couldn't wait for the next day to practice on my four best friends, Miguel, Wings, Coolie Tony and cousin Wayney James! I had already delighted them with my mastery of putting all the expletives together in one single sentence. I was good!

At age eleven two events unfolded and my world was dramatically changed. I became me. Papa had a stroke which paralyzed the left side of his body. He could not move. His left side was dead and his face twisted to one side. Every evening I would run all the way from Providence Primary School, to plop my bag on his feet, anxiously waiting for his grunt. Nothing, no response, he just looked at me, trying to smile from one side of his face. It made him look funny and I would wipe away the drool that followed. My grandmother would be busy between managing the grocery shop she operated, cooking and doing other chores. Somehow she never bothered me to help her and just waited on my other cousins to arrive home. She would just bring me Papa's dinner and soon we settled into a routine, and I would feed Papa.

A week or so into that routine I came home from school to see my grandfather all dressed in new plaid pajamas I had not seen before. A beautiful woman I had also never seen before was feeding him. My grandmother was standing in the room and everyone, even my grandfather looked very happy. My grandmother said, "punky, come hug ur mother". Mother? Did mama say mother as in M.O.T.H.E.R? This woman standing before me, this lady was my mother. I felt bashful, shy, not sure how to react. I need not have worried because the pretty lady they said was my mother came over and hugged me. She hugged me so tightly, her hair had fallen on my face and I could smell her perfume. She smelled sooo good. My mother, my grandfather's pet child, had come home from England to take care of him when she heard he was ill.

Being an explorer, my grandfather had sent off four of his children, including my mother, in the many waves of migrants to England. They all left behind their children for my grandparents to raise and nurture. My cousins Bibs and Neicey were my uncle's children, while Sally and I were from two sisters. I was two years old when my mother left so I had no recollection of her. Anyway, here she was, hugging me as if her life depended on it. Later in the evening I watched mesmerized as she applied her makeup; carefully she made a line over her eyebrows, heavy mascara followed, then it was rouge on her cheeks before finally some red lipstick. Her complexion was flawless. If I had thought her pretty before, I was mistaken, my mother, was as gorgeous as a movie star. I couldn't wait for school the following day to tell my friends and all the students within earshot, and for them to see her.

The following day I raced home from school even faster than before to see my mother and grandfather. And there she was, sitting on the bed feeding my grandfather who already looked so much healthier. This time my mother looked even prettier as she was already dressed to go out. She was going out and awaiting friends to pick her up. She told Papa she would be back later and beckoned me to follow her. I couldn't be more happy. Me and my pretty mommy were going out together. I hoped my friends would see us. Out of the earshot of my grandfather, my mother asked me to sit down. She told me how proud she was of my grades in school and asked me if I knew the meaning of secret. I nodded yes, wondering where this conversation was going. Why was I not putting on one of the pretty dresses she had brought from England for me? Looking me straight in the eye, my mother asked me to keep a secret, just between us. I was bursting with happiness. My mother trusted me to keep her secret. I excitedly said, yes mommy, yes! "Mmm..." said my mother. "That's the first part of the secret, do not call me mommy... don't tell anyone I am your mother. I love you, but I am too young to have an 11 year old child."

I am unable to describe the rejection I felt. It was too late to keep that secret as I had already told the entire Providence Primary School my mother was visiting from England. Not believing me that this pretty woman was my mother, Jenny Findlay the loud speaker in my group of friends, saw my mother and her friends on the main road one day and proceeded up to her. My tear-filled pleas to not ask her anything made my friends, including Betty Fuller my bestie, doubt my story even more. So to show me up, they stopped my mother and boldly asked… "Good evening maam, Punky say that you is her mother, is true?" While I prayed for the earth to swallow my little body, my mother turned purple before finally nodding yes. The beating she gave me later concretized the importance of keeping secrets.

I believe my grandmother never told Papa the reason for the beating she heard I had gotten from my mother. Somehow he still knew, and when my grandmother asked my mother when she would be leaving, no one looked at his pained expression. This was his pet child, and her visit had improved his health, so she must have done something for her mother - my grandmother - to hurry her departure. My grandmother prayed all the time, and in her prayer now she asked God to help her daughter to be a better person. My relationship with my grandmother changed and she became more tolerant of me; she waited on me until I found my shoes, dirty socks and clothes for us to go together to church. She would spontaneously kiss me and tell me she loved me. One day she said, "Punky, what you think of the church people down the road, who always preach dat God work miracles, you think we should ask dem to pray for u papa?" The request was strange, only because Mama worshipped at the Catholic Church, and now that her husband was paralyzed, she was going to the Pentecostal, roadside, clap hand, loud shouting, Church for help.

The pastor, Elder Roberts agreed to come with his Deacon and other prayer healers. He instructed my grandmother to fast on that day, and to also ensure Papa fasted. That evening I would witness my first miracle. The church prayed and commanded my grandfather to move, in the name of Jesus. They shouted if he believed in the power of God, he would be healed. After hours of praying and with the members drenched in sweat, I saw my grandfather move his paralyzed left leg, then he moved it over some more until he was able to stand up. I watched transfixed as my Papa stood up, through the power of the most high God Jehovah. My belief and my faith in God's divine power was sealed. My grandfather regained his mobility and walked with a cane for the next three years before he died.

I am grateful. My grandfather taught me the value of reading, gender equality, religious awareness, understanding of the social inequities and how they affect people's lives. My Papa was convinced that education was the only way out of poverty, to enable the poor to become 'somaddy". Being somebody, would give you the respect and justice that was your natural birthright, not dependent on race, skin shade and location of birth. Most importantly my grandfather taught me the power of faith in God and his ability to work miracles even on those who were not church-goers. Before his stroke, my grandfather was a good man who believed in God. But his experience made him a testament of God's divine power.

My grandmother taught me to pray, to be kind and forgiving. She was a Roman Catholic but her relationship with God was never bound by religion. Mama's was an example of spiritual connectedness with the one God. She could not read but never allowed that to define her. I will always remember the many times she stood up for what was fair and just. She taught me forgiveness. Being rejected by my mother was fundamental in making me the mother I am to my biological children, my three stepchildren from my previous marriage, and my two 'adopted' children. I never want for any child to experience that level of rejection.

I am grateful for the empathy, passion and spirituality Papa and Grandma demonstrated which prepared me to cry, bawl and laugh with the people with whom I work. I am grateful they showed the way to go beyond our call of duty to help individuals and communities. I now recognize how my childhood weekends spent in the rum bar with my grandfather shaped and sharpened my life's perspectives, religious ideology, social awareness, and eventually my chosen path. I credit all I am today to those weekly bar visits and discussions. The work I do, the interventions, are aligned with how I was raised, with my being, my purpose, with who and all that I am.

THAT ADDRESS
(1993)

That Address (1993)

Tick... tick... tick... The steady rhythm of the clock breaks the silence of the office. The stillness magnifies the absence of the organization's accustomed routine. It is an unusual occurrence for our health clinic and community hub.

Usually at 9 am, the entire place, clinic and hallways, would be packed to capacity with impatient mothers with anxious faces and crying babies kotched on their hips demanding a number. A number was a prized possession. It ensured the women were registered and would be subsequently seen by the nurse or doctor in the order that matched the time of their arrival at the clinic. A scattering of young fathers would be pacing the corridors, stopping every now and then to check on the number given to their 'baby mothers'.

Only thirty numbers were assigned for each clinic session. Everyone knew that, so coming early and receiving a number was quite an achievement. The ones without numbers would sit quietly. They knew the wait would be long, maybe all day. They came anyway, with the usual 'cheese trix' in hand for the babies to snack on while they waited. They reasoned it was better to wait in their community clinic than experience the same waiting period at the public clinic downtown.

But the clinic situation had changed to a new scenario, much to the consternation of the residents and distress of the organization's staff. For the past three weeks there had been no immunization clinic. Mothers were forced to fork out money they did not have for bus fares to make their way downtown to the nearest health clinic. They also had to pay a fee for the services downtown.

Prior to the immunization clinic closing, a Peace Corp volunteer, "Nurse Sarah" as she was affectionately called, used to take whatever money they had as a contribution. Nurse Sarah was never so busy that she could not stop to briefly chit chat with each mother and play with their babies. She had provided invaluable service to our clinic for three years, but her tenure ended and was not renewable. The community had sadly bid her farewell two weeks before and she was already greatly missed by the community members and staff.

Finding a replacement, and more so a local person, to provide the service of a qualified registered nurse in the inner-city community was proving even more difficult than we had anticipated. We placed three well-positioned, expensive advertisements for a registered nurse in the most recognized media outlet. They proved to be ineffective in luring potential candidates, except for a sprinkling of calls to ask about the clinic's location. There was a noticeable pattern. "Kingston 13? Where is this please?" the callers would cautiously ask. Most would politely wait for a pause in the middle of the sentence of our explanation to hang up. Some were not so polite and abruptly hung up at the beginning of the word "Wal". We were never able to finish the words "Waltham Park"…"Wal" provided enough information to end the conversation.

The clinic was located in one of Kingston's communities known for many ills including a high homicide rate, teenage pregnancy and high unemployment. It wasn't unusual for staff members and residents to be challenged in finding taxis that were willing to transport them into the community. Gender played a huge role in the perception of safety. Males, especially young men who were not residents in the community, did not enter without being accompanied by relatives or friends known to the community. The absence of the usual clinic, the resulting silence and the difficulty recruiting new staff gave our organization a greater sense of the residents' cry - the stifling effects of the stigma they faced daily.

As my thoughts returned to the stillness of the empty clinic, I am reminded of Damion and his visit of two weeks before.

"Ms. Angie, somebody is here to see you, can I show him in?" Lilieth, the secretary asked. I looked up and my eyes were immediately locked with eyes of pain and frustration. The eyes were Damion's, a young man who we had come to know because of the countless recommendations we had written to help him in his pursuit of work. Damion was quiet and reserved, yet exhibited a friendly personality. Much to his mother's and his community's joy, he had graduated a year before, achieving passes in seven Caribbean Examination Council (CXC) subjects. That number of subjects meant he could compete for University acceptance or for jobs.

He sat and fidgeted with a rag in his hand, twisting it around his fingers and fighting to compose himself. I waited, making small talk, to which he only nodded. He sipped the water the secretary brought in for him and twisted the rag some more. He furtively looked behind him, then got up and closed the door, locking us both in from the inside. His chair made a scraping noise on the floor as he dragged it so the desk did not separate us and he could sit close to me. "Ms. Angie", he whispered, "me have something a want to tell you." I nodded in encouragement and he continued, "Ms. Angie, I am cousin to Tony, the yute that dead last week, and when I see how my aunty a bawl I don't want that for me, it coulda be me..."

I tried to interrupt, to tell him he was different, to remind him he had chosen a different path from his cousin and was a success story, achieving seven CXC. He had options, be patient, I told him. We would help… he was a good boy and had made his mother proud. "Nooo, nooo," he cried, "my modda proud becaaz she don't know what me doin." He paused and looked straight at me. "Miss Angie, me not good like how you and everybody tink." He swallowed and with a deliberate, slow voice he forced out the words he had come to say. "Miss Angie, I am the locker, a me lock de gun dem fi de Crescent gang!"

The words penetrated my brain and took on their meaning. Damion, you, a locker? I knew what locker meant, but surely Damion must be joking. I sought clarity. I asked, "you mean… you put away the guns, hide dem from police and other gunman?" With serious calmness, he responded, "Yes, Miss Angie, me in charge of inventory fi de guns, me in charge of inventory fi de shots and me in charge of renting, issuing and getting back all inventory on the streets." I was shocked. How long had he held this position? How did he get involved? He said, "Miss Angie, when I was fifteen, one day police raid the community and order all de yute dem to face the wall and search dem. Dem search all the yute on the corner except for me. Them run me home to my madda. The man dem see that and decide that me have a innocent face, I am always going school with knapsack, so I must carry de guns for them when they moving from one ends to the other. But as mi get older and them see how I can do accounts, they step up the task an ask me to check off on goods. Gradually me get responsibility to do all checking off, because dem know I am not involve, so they don't have to worry. I will take any stock, no bullet will be missing. Don't worry doah, Miss Angie, I never use one yet, that's why I get the position, they know I don't and would never use a gun, and they don't want me to." There was a pause before he went on, "Miss Angie, me waan stop, but can't even get a job, every time I apply for something I know I qualify for, them look at my address, see that it's Kingston 13, then tell me they will call. They never call. What a must do?"

"What a must do?" a question echoing the realities for the community's youth, especially male youth. It was now also our organization's awakening reality, as we were unable to attract qualified persons to fill a much needed job in the community in the same way that residents and in particular young males like Damion, who were educated and qualified, were unable to find work because of their address.

A month after we advertised for a nurse, the neighboring St. Peter Claver Church informed us that a registered nurse was among their new batch of volunteers and would be assigned to our clinic. The news that our clinic would soon have a nurse spread throughout the lanes like wildfire on dry mountains. Some said it was their prayers that were answered and they would pray some more that she would be like Nurse Sarah. Others were skeptical; no one would be as nice as Nurse Sarah, but it was ok, she would be welcome. Having a nurse would result in the resumption of our holistic health services: preventative health care, nutrition, immunization to babies, blood pressure clinic for the elderly and more. The babies with the telltale signs of Kwashiorkor—red hairline, large tummies on small frames and sharp protruding knees— would be attended to. A nurse on board was one of the most important aspects of our organization's functioning, enabling us to fulfill our vision and purpose of helping community members achieve improved health and reduce non-communicable diseases.

The ticking of the clock brings me back to the present. It's now Monday and we are finally ready to meet our new nurse. It feels like D-Day and for the umpteenth time I glance at the clock centered on the wall in the middle of the office. It is 9:40 am. Only ten minutes have passed since my last glance. The secretary leafs through the monthly report trying to appear engrossed but the tap-tap of the pen in her hand tells another story. Her furtive glances at the clock confirm her unease. The telephone rings and her expression lights up like a light bulb. She grabs it by the second ring but the look of excitement immediately gives way to disappointment. The call is for the education department. She mechanically puts the call through and twirls the pen. Meanwhile, I can't concentrate enough to prioritize my tasks. I listen for the nurse's entrance. The interview had been scheduled for 9:00 am sharp.

The pile of papers and folders on my desk signifies the many things to do and heightens my anxiety. The education department is due for a monitoring visit. An urgent meeting with the community council is needed to plan the upcoming visit of an important international donor. Then there are the two drop-ins sitting outside the hallway demanding urgent attention.

One is Miss Cherry, whose situation has become familiar to the staff. Frequent beatings from her common-law husband prompt visits in which she is allowed the privacy and environment to vent her fears, anger, frustrations and be listened to without judgment. She in turn listens to us, quietly, respectfully, nodding her head at the right time, making the appropriate sounds to show the reasoning resonates with her "hmmm, mmm, mm, a chue, mmmm, yes mam." She will return home, back to her world, calmer, resolute, even if no decision is made. There are the children to think of, her ego, the other women, or "matey" waiting in line ready to laugh at her, waiting on their opportunity to move in on the coveted position, being the woman of the house, wifey! For the time being, she will take the beating, save her nest egg and entertain fantasies of killing him... but not yet.

Waiting outside too is Maas Joseph, an elderly gentleman who does not trust anyone apart from the staff to read the letters his daughter writes to him from the UK. No! He declines suggestions for a more accessible reader. The neighbors are too inquisitive and much too "beggy, beggy" he says. Reading his letters will reveal private details of his daughter's life: they will know she is not straight, not legal and is working under the table. They will know she is not as rich as she looks in the photos he shows everyone. More importantly they will know his financial affairs that he is sure will attract unwanted attention.

Together the two sit in the foyer, each watching the other and waiting on their turn to be called in to see me. It is hard to determine between the community members and myself, who better enjoys the open-door policy I have established. For two days, Mondays and Thursdays, community members can walk in without appointment for counselling, advice, to share current social and political news, or just to say hello. Today should have been no different, but it is. They understand, and so patiently, they too wait on the nurse's arrival.

The recurring question jumps around, "Where is this nurse?" Americans are usually punctual; late is considered disrespectful, especially if they are going for a job interview. An American Catholic volunteer nurse would not be willingly late. Something is not quite right, but what?

"Lilieth!" I call to the secretary, "any telephone call, any word to explain the nurse's lateness?" Anxiety has now turned onto Worry Street, which heads straight on to Speculation Boulevard. My theories move at a chaotic pace. Maybe there is a change in the Church's plans to send a nurse to work in our community? And what of the Nurse? Has the nurse heard of the address of this assignment and has had second thoughts?

Suddenly the stillness is broken by a commotion in the corridor and an angry outburst. "What kind-a place is this? Where is Ms. Aaangela?" the words betray a distinct American accent. Frightened, the secretary and I look across the room at each other and in one accord we scurry outside to see the source of the noise. In front of us stands a tall disheveled looking man, shirt ripped wide open and barely covering a section of his arms. His beige pants are covered in dirt and both his shoes have somehow lost their laces. He glares angrily at the persons sitting in the waiting area. Miss Cherry shoots the intruder a look of anger and Maas Joseph inches away on the bench. The intruder is a dark-skinned man, his accent indicating an African American. He is tall and has the body of a heavy weight boxer. He turns at the sound of my entrance and fixes his glare on me as he demands, "Wheyre's Ms. Aaangela?"

I assume my most professional voice. "Hello, how may I help you?" I inquire as I extend my right hand to his. He ignores my outreached hand and squints at me looking up and down and back to my face. I later learn he cannot see well without the aid of his glasses. "They mugged me!" he shouts, "the hoodlums jumped me. I put up a fight, as you can see I ain't no chicken, but there were four of them, so they kinda got the better of me, took ma gold chain, ma waallet, ma glasses and ma daam phone!" His voice gets louder and angrier with each sentence. Community members inside the clinic come up the staircase. The place is now jammed and everyone is talking at once. He has to shout even louder to be heard, "I was coming down to see you, for the interview you know. I'm Michael, the church sent me to help y'all, and this is how you treat me. Maaan!!" It takes a minute for me to register the information. This man is the nurse! The registered nurse we are waiting for! Someone has made an error on the paperwork; he is Michael and not Michelle.

Michael had clearly not followed his briefing notes. International volunteers are usually briefed and prepared for their entry into the community. The briefing provides contextual information on the community background, social, political and economic situation and issues of cultural sensitivity. This includes the volunteer's attire and image management, community perception, relationship and acceptance. The standard advice: no brash display of wealth, jewelry, brand name clothing and accessories; limited display of body parts even if the weather/sun is at its highest to eliminate overt sexuality, especially applicable to females. The young man in front of me had defied the advice. Michael had worn expensive brand name clothes and was decked out with jewelry. Being African American, his attire made him look like a wealthy Jamaican from overseas, or a local person involved in illegal drug activities. He did not fit the community's image of an international volunteer.

The community had become accustomed to international volunteers and local visitors of all races, ethnicities and religious backgrounds. They were well aware of our organization's partnership with international agencies and the need to sometimes show the impact of partners' investments. They welcomed partners in their homes and understood this to be a function of the social development process. As such, each visitor and volunteer was protected with fierce loyalty. Volunteers were usually easily recognized for their simple style of dressing, their behaviors and because they were usually white. Michael did not fit the perceived image of a volunteer; his clothes and identity as an African American distorted the community's perception. Other African American volunteers we had hosted were recognized as "foreigner" and treated with the loyalty and respect given to volunteers. However, Michael's display of his jewelry, his clothes and pointed shoes fit the image of a rich Jamaican and made him a target for easy picking.

Father Bruce, the resident Catholic priest, responded immediately to our SOS call. A Canadian Jesuit, Father Bruce lived among the people in a modest dwelling. He was tall with eyes as blue as the sky and pale white skin that refused to absorb a tan regardless of his daily walks through the community in the hot sun. He immediately took responsibility for not fully briefing Michael and together we attempt to calm him. Our apologies are no good. Neither is our promise that given time we could retrieve his stolen goods.

The promise is met with an unbelieving stare and loud outburst. Michael wishes to leave immediately and go back to his guesthouse in the nice up-scale area of Kingston 6. An interview will not be necessary - out of the question, he declares. He could not consider working in the community, for the residents were uncouth, primitive and he could not serve them.

At Michael's request a taxi comes. With what was left of his shirt held in hand, and head held high he gets in the taxi and off he goes, back to what he considered civilization.

It was not a proud day. As an organization, we worked with the community to try to break the stigma that outsiders had and to fulfill the organization's mission to help residents transform their address into one of which they could be proud. The incident meant that we had to act to redeem the organization's name and what we stood for, and the reputation of the broader community as well. We knew we had to engage the community to resolve the issue.

News of the nurse's hurried departure reverberates throughout the community, into the yards and through the cracks into the homes. "Dem rab the nurse! The buoy dem up de road rab the nurse. Lawd Gad, them rab the nurse!!" The community is in shock, and people respond even more angrily than Michael. The sight of Michael with shirt in hand sitting in the back of the speeding taxi fuels outrage.

The don from the lower end of the road comes up, followed by his entourage of over fifteen gun-happy youth. They want the clinic's confirmation. Is the rumor they have heard true? Did the boys at the top of the road really disrespect and violate the clinic's honor and rob the nurse? The nurse who is coming to help them, to provide them with condoms, to look after their baby mothers, their babies and their own mothers. Did they really violate the unwritten code of conduct to give safe passage to the organization's staff and volunteers? Our confirmation brings immediate consequences. War is declared! Our cries for peace, for discussion with the perpetrators, fall on deaf ears. They want blood.

It takes hours of pleading by Father Bruce and I, reasoning, highlighting biblical teachings and anecdotes that they can relate to, before we are able to get through to the consciousness of the don and his entourage. They relent, under two conditions: one, the don in charge of the perpetrators must carry out internal justice, or they would. Two, within 24 hours everything stolen must be returned and the nurse be at work!

We are visibly petrified, traumatized and some of us cry openly. Working in the inner-city, our staff and volunteers have become accustomed to sporadic gang war. This time it is different and the cause of it provokes trembling among the hardest hearts among us. The dons have declared war to defend our honor, the "Clinic's" honor. The gangs see it as an opportunity to demonstrate their love and their loyalty, to protect us and all who work at the clinic. They are prepared to kill each other in our name. The priest is equally shaken; the purpose and possible outcomes of this war have not escaped him. This is a nightmare.

Members of the community, mostly females and elderly males, have stayed to express their outrage and give their support to the nurse who had by then already left. Together we hold each other's hands. We are Christians of diverse denominations, Rastafarian, and Muslim. We form a circle. With bowed heads and fingers gripping tightly, we make a large circle in the middle of the road and pray. We pray to the God of Abraham. We pray like there is no tomorrow. The women pray for their sons and family who may be affected by the potential war. We pray and then pray some more.

Early the next morning, Father Bruce and his assistant join the staff at the clinic. Residents from all sections of the community join. Puffed eyes and nervous smiles are on every face. The staff sit apprehensively staring and making small talk. There is no attempt to pretend they are busy. People walk by the clinic and the ones who have witnessed the fight between Michael and the yutes retell their version. It has been 24 hours and we are waiting for the Crescent Road don to call us. There is talk of youth trying to run away from the community, being held, hand cuffed and led down the lane. It is approximately 9:30 am. Two youth enter the clinic, and everyone looks expectantly at them. They survey the room and purposefully walk towards me and the priest. They inform us of their task. It is simple. They are here to take us to the 'Justice yard'. Would we come with them please? The entire staff and community members in the room get up to follow them. They look at the residents and staff as parents look at naughty children and shake their head in exasperation. No, they say, only four persons must accompany them, a crowd is not necessary. Father Bruce requests his assistant's presence, and I select Glen, a staff member. He is a young man and is street smart, once a gangster who had changed his life and was now a role model and mentor to our youth population. We are ready. With hearts beating loudly we follow the two youth like dutiful children.

The lanes we go through are narrow; board houses and zinc fences are on either side and only two persons can walk side by side. There are sometimes ditches and we maneuver our way around them making a long line. There is no pretense of conversation; we are too scared at what we will see to speak. It's time to be still, to be quiet and pray. We have no idea of our destination, the location they have designated where their version of justice is to be carried out. Justice Yard can be anywhere, secluded and never repeated for diverse reasons: fear of police knowing the location and setting an ambush; privacy from community residents' interference; and the ability to have a broad vision of oncoming persons without lookouts being detected. We walk through lanes and gullies until we arrive in a big yard. We are directed to the back. With hearts thumping to a scared rhythm, we proceed.

We come upon four youth on the ground. They are all in kneeling positions, and their hands dangle out of shape in front of them. There is blood all over them and my heart bleeds with their blood. I know them all and one of them has eyes so swollen he surely is unable to see us. He is Damion, the youth who visited the office two weeks ago. He has a phone in his right hand and does not look up at me. One of the youth clutches a wallet with bloody hands, while another uses trembling hands in a vain attempt to repair the broken frame of a pair of glasses. All four immediately begin to speak at once to us. The don, a short light-skinned youth with a skinny frame, places his finger to his lips and there is utter silence. He points to one youth as a gesture allowing only him to speak.

The youth with the bloody hands begins to speak. He apologizes for his behavior, for the group's behavior, he wants to apologize to the nurse in person. They made a mistake in his identity. He explains, "Father, we woulda neva touch him if we did know him was a nurse, him look like one a we, a druggist, he never look like a foriner much less a nurse. Please, Miss Angie, please Father, forgive we. We never mean to disrespect the clinic." They explain that when they heard he was the nurse assigned to the clinic they never even bothered to open the wallet. All his money and credit cards were left untouched. They just needed a small screwdriver to repair the glasses they had broken in the fight with him. One says his mother is a dressmaker, could the nurse bring the shirt so she could sew it back together, he asks. The apologies go on and on.

The youth are remorseful. The don informs us it is our decision how they will carry out further justice. They could send them home to meet their savior, or we could have them beaten again. It is the invitation we are waiting for to step into our role as priest, counsellor, social change agents. Logwood is gathered and placed on top of concrete blocks to create chairs so we can sit in a circle. Father Bruce prays for their lives: that they make wise choices, turn their lives around to be good young men, and never to give in to temptation. But how, they ask? We listen as they relate their economic conditions, their aspirations; we listen as Damion relates that he has tried many times to get jobs he knew he was qualified for but was told the position was filled when the interviewer heard his address. Other youth use Damion's experience as an example of an unfair system to youth: what is the use of education if your address is the first thing they see?

The don listens in respectful silence as we challenge them about their own role in sealing doors already half closed with stories like yesterday's robbery. We allow them to process thoughts of the far-reaching, long-term repercussions of their actions and how such actions facilitate and reinforce discrimination against them and the community. We argue that coping with the stigma of their address ultimately means they must be better; not be mediocre at whatever skills they embark on, but instead be the best plumbers, the best carpenters. We applaud Damion for his achievement in passing seven subjects in school and reaffirm hope that if he goes to a community college and gains accreditation and/or additional subjects it would increase his competitive edge. We challenge those who have dropped out of school and lack the basic Grade 9 level of achievement. We challenge them on why they were not enrolled in a skills program. To this the unanimous response was '"no money, Miss Angie, no money Father Bruce, no money to pay for these courses, no money for bus fare and lunch, so we hustle." We leave the meeting with the distinct feeling they will not rob someone again. For now.

The other dons of the community are satisfied justice has been served. They understand the code of conduct had not been violated. It was an identity mix-up. Each don is secretly happy their gang members were not the ones who had made the mistake.

Father Bruce is dumbfounded. He has ministered in several of Jamaica's toughest neighborhoods and boasts of having served in some of Canada's poorest. He believes he has seen and done it all. But not this, according to him. "Angela, never have I seen anyone get robbed, the perpetrators apologize, return all the goods and make amends to repair what was broken." We lapse into silence as we walk back. What could we do to enhance the youths' opportunities for jobs, to compete with candidates whose addresses did not induce fear among potential employers? As a strategy to gain employment many applicants have changed addresses on their resume and job application forms. "Mmm," says the priest in perfect patois, "Donkey say de world no level, it no level fe chue."

Father Bruce and I return Michael's belongings and convey to him the youths' apologies. He mumbles something about thugs under his breath, while he vigorously wipes his gold chain. We stand awkwardly as he wipes for about ten minutes, examines and then wipes again before placing it over his neck. He punches each number of the keys of his mobile phone. Satisfied that it works he places it in the phone case on his hip. He then opens his wallet and slowly counts his money —it's a mixture of Jamaican and US currency. His face involuntarily twitches into a smile. The smile does not last. The frame on his glasses is not properly repaired; he indignantly points to the dirt on his wallet. No, he would not consider working with hoodlums. There is no guarantee he would not be robbed again.

I listen to Michael rant and feel a wave of disappointment. Despite his claim of worldly exposure and Christian belief, Michael lacks empathy, the ability to put in context the experience, use it as a learning opportunity and forgive. Robberies are not a uniquely Jamaican experience; robberies are unfortunate situations that happen in all major cities and parts of the world. But where else would the outcome have been as it was in the Waltham inner-city community? An apology and return of goods. That is unique.

A week later, a young Jamaican nurse responded to the advertisement and requested directions to the clinic. "Yes," Lilieth reiterated for the tenth time, "yes, the young lady was aware the clinic is located in Kingston 13, and yes, she was still interested." The young woman, "Nurse Barbara" as we would come to know her, was a staunch Catholic and heard of the available position through the Catholic grapevine. Nurse Barbara, unfazed by the address, began working the following Monday morning and soon became a household name. Nurse Barbara would serve the S-Corner Clinic in the Waltham community for another twenty years.

The situation with Damion provoked our organization to review our programs and what we could do, in a practical way, to support youth like him to access jobs and keep them out of the gang culture that reinforces the community's stigma. Out of the bad came much good.

The don, in his show of support for a different future for Damion, quietly replaced his position with a new "locker". Father Bruce was impressed with Damion's academic achievement and provided the financial support for him to pursue an accounting degree at an impressive college. The idea to provide sponsorship to youth with the aptitude for further education and/or vocational skills training was thus born and blossomed into a life of its own. The Church led by Father Bruce became the first sponsor for this aspect of our second chance educational program. Our organization would later forge relationships with private funders to further enhance this career development program. The educational program was extended from being a one-year course that helped school dropouts to achieve a Grade 9 level and high school certification, to include a mandatory vocational skills training program. Each student was guaranteed the financial sponsorship for a skills training program. Every year an average of twenty youth, male and female, were placed in a vocational skills program for their chosen career.

The program lifted the hope of many of the youth who once believed that they would never be able to fulfill their aspirations for a better life and that their only chance of survival was through petty robbery or hustling, being on the street corner kneading their palms with ganja to make a spliff and light up. The program provided an alternative to the streets and antisocial activities.

Our network would later facilitate the opportunity for Damion to be considered for an accounting position in an established food chain. But it was Damion's performance, integrity and ambition that would propel him up the corporate ladder to become one of their accounting managers.

Damion provided mentorship to many community youth in our program and became the symbol reinforcing the importance of education and hard work. He became a role model to youth witnessing his transformation. He has since moved out of the community, married and is raising his family. Up to the time of writing Damion remains committed to making a difference in young people's lives. He is the president of his community's citizen association which includes a youth club in which he serves as a mentor.

WOMAN POWAH
(1995)

Woman Powah (1995)

The tantalizing aroma of curried chicken-back seeps out of the huge dutch-pot (*round aluminum cooking pot*) sitting in a stately position on piles of cackling wood fire. The aroma travels up the road, across the open land and down the road. It is an oversized pot. Beside it, and giving its aroma stiff competition, are two equally large pots. As every hot beverage is called 'tea', this chocolate tea is bubbling and makes popping sounds. A film of oil shimmers on the top. The other pot, a blackened kerosene tin, has white flour dumplings and green bananas dancing around as they cook.

Men with sweaty faces and soaked t-shirts hover around the wood fire stoves with chipped mugs in their hands. Ms. Delores, the head cook, stands guarding the pots with arms akimbo at her waist. They approach her pot. "The tea not ready yet, go away, oono too craven!" She shoos them away waving her hands wildly in front of her, her gestures dramatic and effective. The men shrug in exasperation before turning back to their tasks.

Ms. Delores ignores their loud, disgruntled sighs and turns back to the immediate task at hand. She removes logs from the heap the children made to add to the crackling fire. She then uses a big wooden spoon to stir the boiling chocolate tea, adding sweetened condensed milk and grated nutmeg. The men watch her. She lifts the spoon to her mouth, blows on it to cool the liquid before spilling it onto the palm of her hand to taste. She stands still, smacks her lips loudly and groans in delight at her culinary skill. "Mmm! Yes. Oono come now." The men quickly heed and diligently form a line. Maas Brim, Ms. Delores' assistant, cuts hard-dough bread into slices before scooping a large spoonful of callaloo on one side. He places another slice on top, making callaloo sandwiches. He tells the hungry men in the line to come for their sandwiches after getting their tea. Other workers, unmindful of the tea-break, continue the task of laying concrete blocks in the three-foot hole that they had dug early that morning.

It is National Labor Day in Jamaica, a day when people come together to give voluntary labor for causes they strongly support. Under our Organization's stewardship, the Community Development Council (CDC) decided on the Labor Day project, and news of the project, the purpose and the beneficiary travelled throughout the neighborhood grapevine. The project: construction of a one-bedroom self-contained home for Marcia.

Marcia was one of the most popular and admired young women in the community. She had a caramel colored complexion, petite body and an easy smile that filled her oval face. Marcia had gained popularity because of her open defiance of the unwritten rules of dating and relationships. She had chosen a partner from the rival section on the other side of the border line, who would become her baby father. She had met her Joe at age 15, when they both attended the same high school that served the community and adjoining neighborhoods. Joe soon dropped out of school and was recruited into a gang. Soon he was wanted by the gangs in the section of the community where Marcia had lived all her life. With total oblivion to the risk of being together, the two became inseparable. They kept the relationship a secret, but Marcia would quietly meet Joe in his section of the community. His neighbors knew her, and her witty stories of how she dodged the gangs and even her brother to get there made them laugh. The elderly residents loved her for her defiance to pursue love, and in turn, Joe's peer group revered him for his boldness in taking a woman from the rival gang.

News of Marcia's pregnancy at age 16 generated minimal attention. The national concern over increased teenage pregnancies was not reflected at the local community level. Being mindful of this accepted norm, our health department advocated and promoted family and parenting programs to reduce this subculture. It was the news of who the baby father was that traveled with alarming alacrity and created apprehension and excitement. Marcia's pregnancy solidified her alliance with Joe's section of the community and now opened her to new risk. While women generally were not targets in gang war, the woman of a shooter was and could be used as a means to send horrific, revengeful messages through rape, beatings or even murder. Residing in the opposing community to her baby father, Marcia could also be branded an "informa" (one who takes secrets from one side to the other). The brand "informa" was one of the most feared names that could be assigned to an individual, and knowing her family ties could not save her from either fate, Marcia was forced to flee her home. Joe's community welcomed her as an honorary citizen and there she resided up to the time of the beating which almost cost her life.

Marcia was now 23 years old, the mother of four children, and unfortunately had become a victim of severe domestic abuse. Our organization came to know her through her attendance at the health clinic. She was a regular at the health center, her visits alternating between the family planning clinics for contraceptives, the prenatal clinic when the contraceptives failed, and the administration office to see me for one-on-one domestic abuse counseling. Marcia exhibited the telltale signs of domestic abuse: unexplained swollen face and body parts and her nervous, inconsistent responses when questioned. The clinic referred Marcia to our domestic abuse program, which like many other abused women, she never attended. The women usually opted for one-to-one sessions, and as such I became her confidante. Marcia confided her fear of Joe who was now an infamous gangster and she feared for her life should she leave him. He had a quick temper, which was exaggerated whenever he was broke. She suspected he was cheating, and the arguments escalated into physical fights. One of those fights resulted in her being hospitalized for almost a week with fractured ribs and bruises. She wished desperately to leave him but where would she go? Over and over her questions spilled out: would the section of the community that she had fled from eight years ago accept her return to live among them? Could she still be a target, even though she had left Joe? Moreover, how would she support herself and four children? She had dropped out of school because of pregnancy, had no skills by which to earn and depended totally on Joe for financial support. How would she manage without Joe's support?

Domestic violence, in which married or common-law spouses beat or rape their partners, is rampant and an accepted norm in many inner-city communities. This in no way suggests that domestic violence is exclusive to the inner-city, as it cuts across all strata of the Jamaican society. 'Above the Crossroads clock' men in suits beat their tea-party going, stiletto-wearing wives with the same enthused vigor and self-appointed power within the confines of their gated mansions. The victims generally display similar behaviors of denial of their situation.

Women Health Survey 2016, UN Women—"Her husband holds a prominent position, functioning as lay preacher and deacon... "I moved out of the main bedroom to the guest room. After a few days, and after prayers, he came in and wanted sex. I refused and he locked the doors so the children could not hear and he had his way with me. I felt raped and violated. I got over it because I reflected on the fact that he is my husband but I am still angry to this day. In the morning, we both went to work as if nothing happened."

According to Country Reports on Human Rights, violence against women continues to be a serious problem in Jamaica, but many women are still reluctant to acknowledge or report abusive behavior, leading to significant variations in reported prevalence...

The acceptance of domestic violence in relationships as a way of life influences neighbors to look the other way and not to intervene unless they believe the situation to be life threatening.

At the community level, abuse often includes the use of weapons—knives and guns—in addition to the physical aggression leading to broken bones, bruising or swollen limbs. Domestic abuse creates a dichotomy as victims' shame often causes them to avoid the very help they need and so inadvertently challenges our organization's efforts to facilitate support programs.

Women of the community do not laugh at each other even when there is conflict between them otherwise. Silent empathy for the physical and emotional beating they experience is shared among the women. Everyone knows the victims, knows the other's story, and many have experienced physical or sexual abuse by their spouse. Nonetheless they do not attend the counselling sessions which would bring them together for collective support. When questioned, the typical response from women experiencing abuse is, "We (meaning she and her spouse) don't really have a problem, is just a lickle misunderstanding we have becaz..." They then expand on the reasons they believe triggered and justified their spouse's action, at times blaming themselves for something they may have said or done.

The causes of domestic violence are complex and varied but generally are found to be the power dynamics within the relationships, dependence, unemployment, finances, cheating, women's reproductive health and her role as caregiver. This is a complex set of factors that our health department aimed to address each day as women, often with their children, came to our clinic for help.

The domestic issues that the women faced were not disconnected from the many social, economic and environmental factors impacting their communities and their lives. For example, an alarming increase in communicable diseases among the children of the community led our organization to solicit the Ministry of Health's intervention. The ministry carried out intensive research which revealed the community's very limited sanitation infrastructure and consequently weak sanitation and lifestyle practices. One single pit toilet served as many as five yards, with each yard housing as many as seven families. To further compound the lack of sanitation infrastructure, the community had limited access to a water supply with only three 'standpipes' serving fifty percent of the community. In some sections, residents had hooked up illegal connections to the main pipelines leading to business communities. These conditions weigh heaviest on the women in their multiple roles as care-givers and spouses. Their inability to meet others' expectations in either role often resulted in their physical and psychological abuse.

Understanding the interlinkages contributing to domestic abuse, our organization responded. The published data of the community sanitation and environmental conditions attracted national attention, public outcry and political embarrassment. This was 1994 and an urban community was without water and sanitary convenience. The data magnified the community's alienation, the exclusion from access to basic social services that civil society takes for granted. It facilitated opportunities for donor agency partnerships to urgently respond to the community's squalor. The Environmental Foundation of Jamaica (EFJ) and the Canadian International Development Agency's Green Fund partnered with the clinic to develop and execute a massive sanitation program.

As part of the program, our organization had to revisit how we could best respond to develop programs to facilitate women's empowerment, and at the same time address the health and other needs of children and the broader community.

Mindful that the community was comprised of 54% female-headed households and mindful of the responsibilities placed on all women because of their gender, our organization decided to partner with the Women's Construction Collective to train women in construction skills. We chose to train women in construction to provide them with a skill that would address sanitation in the community. More importantly, this would enhance their opportunities to find employment, have a sustainable income and enable them to make choices for themselves and their families. Marcia was one of these women.

Marcia and twenty-three other women completed training and constructed the first set of Ventilated Improved Pit toilets in Jamaica (VIP). Based on its unique construction qualities, the VIP toilet has two sides with alternating uses: black pipes inserted six feet in the ground facilitate an environmental process that transforms waste to manure. Designed in Uganda and approved by the World Health Organization, the VIP is used in communities without running water to flush. Over an 18-month period, 109 VIP toilets were constructed throughout the community. The toilets were strategically placed in sections where as many as four communal yards could have easy access to sharing an outside toilet.

The sanitation project was a success both for improving health and sanitation practices for the whole community and for building the women's independence. The acquisition of this skill facilitated the women's efforts to earn and support themselves and their children, which in turn empowered them to be able to remove themselves from abusive situations.

During this time Marcia had left her abusive relationship and was now living in her family home. Her earlier fears that she would be a target for the opposing gang members did not materialize, nor did her fear of rejection by family members. A month prior to the National Labor Day, her father Maas Albert had invited staff members to see the layout of his yard, and the spot he had given his daughter Marcia to build her home. The yard had two other houses, a communal toilet our organization had built, and a chicken coop. To accommodate his plans, Maas Albert moved the chicken coop to an unused open lot directly across from his house. He scoffed at our suggestion that he needed the Government's permission to use the land but worried aloud about possible theft of his chickens, declaring, "A just will have to sharpen my machete some more." And so Marcia was assured of a place to construct her home. She cried.

With Labor Day approaching our organization mobilized the human and financial support for the project. The collaboration with the Community Development Council, our most important stakeholder, enabled us to mobilize community volunteers. Food for the Poor, a locally-based organization with international support, provided housing material. The grocery shops provided food and the bakery provided bread. The community provided pots and pans, voluntary labor and music.

In support of and respect for the significance of our Labor Day project, the gangs upheld an unspoken code of conduct across their divided lines. And so, Labor Day saw construction workers regardless of gender, and especially youth, cross over invisible boundaries to lend a helping hand. The strong culture of giving and sharing took precedence over gang feuds. Moreover, this was a community project for someone who everyone knew and loved. Women came out in numbers; women who admired Marcia for her ability to pursue love even when it did not fit within their expectations, to embrace the risk, and to have the strength to leave when it became abusive.

At daybreak on Labor Day, the yard was busy. Construction materials were neatly stacked according to areas of work and people walked around in search of something to do. Time was of the essence and accidents could not be afforded. To ensure this, the community had carried out the traditional ritual of killing a rooster and sprinkling its blood and white rum to enhance the safety and wellbeing of the family who would live in the new house and ward off any negative energies or evil spirits.

This was a well-established ritual practice. Miss Elsie, Marcia's immediate neighbor, donated the oldest and biggest rooster for the sacrifice. The children gleefully chased the rooster around her yard and after much running the screeching rooster was captured and prepared for sacrifice. The men pinned the rooster under an empty paint pan and with one swift chop from a sharpened machete, the protruding head was separated from the body. Miss Maud, a tall bony woman bearing a startling resemblance to the Maasai Tribe in Kenya was known as a prayer warrior. Decked out in bright red turban as usual, she stepped forward to complete the tradition at hand. Miss Maud demanded all eyes be closed and she began to pray. She did not need a mic; her voice rose to a preaching pitch as she prayed aloud while she rocked her upper body sideways to the right and sideways to the left, not once moving her lower body and feet. At the sound of amen from all in the yard, children and adults scampered out of the way as Miss Maud marched towards them with the headless rooster in her right hand and a flask of Wray and Nephew Overproof white rum in the left. We stood at attention as Miss Maud sprinkled the rooster's blood around the four corners of the house. She then took in a mouthful of rum and spewed it in a shower on the four corners. This was followed by another heartfelt prayer for Marcia and her family.

The Labor Day project finally got underway and Marlene, our organization's assistant manager, set about her task to organize persons and resources. She is a tall woman, big in stature and a no-nonsense person who enjoys bossing people around by barking orders. Her naturally loud voice surges above the hammering and chattering to marshal everyone into action—teams directed according to building skills, and materials organized out of the way to allow free movement. Cabinet makers construct customized closets and cupboards; carpenters measure lumber while masons cut through steel for block laying. Cooks are placed in a separate corner away from the hustle and children are given buckets to provide constant water and wood supply. The goal is that by nightfall they will have completed the construction of a one-bedroom home and kitchen for Marcia. The carpenters' hammering makes a smooth rhythm as the nails go into boards that soon are transformed into walls and windows.

The Food for the Poor truck makes several trips with building materials. Youth, both male and female, position themselves in a straight line to pass heavy material from one person to the other until it reaches the designated storage area. Other youth, self-proclaimed electricians, climb up onto the light post to illegally connect electricity for the sound boxes they place at the gate. Soon there will be blaring reggae music, but first the women lead all in the yard in songs of worship, well-known gospel songs. They belt out, "It soon be done, all my troubles and trials. When I get over on the other side... I am gonna shake hands wid de elders, I'm gonna tell all de people good morning I'm gonna sit down beside my Jesus, am gonna sit down an' rest a little while." Marcia cannot contain her emotions any longer. She is overwhelmed by the support of friends, neighbors and family. Tears flow freely down her cheeks.

As a trained mason who built so many latrines for the community, Marcia tries to help the construction of her home but she is more of a hindrance. She is like a happy clumsy child, too excited to contain herself. The beds and other furniture arrive—donations from St. Peter Claver Church and Bethel Baptist Church, led by Pastor Dennis. Reggae music now vibrates throughout the yard, and people dance and sing while they work. The hammering coupled with the command of instructions from the head masons and carpenters create a rhythm of their own. Now and then there are yelps of pain from amateur carpenters who have missed their mark and instead hammered fingers. This ignites great laughter at the victim.

By nightfall the work team is triumphant though weary. Self-taught home decorators show off their skills and move furniture inside and around the home until they receive the onlookers' grunts of approval. Neighbors bring lamps filled with kerosene oil and proudly place them on the middle of the table. The lamps glow as we pray to God to bless the home. We thank him for providing good weather in which to work, and for all who have come out to make the day possible. We glorify God's wonder and grace. I silently thank him for choosing me to lead the organization to carry out his work, empowering women and families for personal and community development and transformation.

Except for the painting and cleaning up of waste material strewn on the ground, Marcia's home is now fully constructed. Marlene, basking in the day's achievement, is already organizing for tomorrow's workday, including skilled volunteer painters and a cleanup crew.

Everyone feels proud. In a true spirit of love, support and sharing, the community, though sometimes torn apart by gang violence, came together to support one of their own. Some of the women who came out were themselves victims of domestic abuse but didn't yet have the strength to leave their own situations. They, were happy for Marcia and took part to facilitate a sister's process for a fresh start, a new beginning. Marcia, once badly abused, had defied the odds: leaving her abuser, acquiring a skill and becoming among the best of our construction workers. Marcia the prodigal child had returned home.

Hard at work - People Count CNN

HARD AT WORK

A tale of two island cities… Kingston, Jamaica and San Juan, Puerto Rico. Both are home to dynamic community leaders who are taking action to ensure that they and their neighbors have better lives.

Barbara Pyle travels to Kingston, where two women are tackling the issues of population growth and poverty in different ways. Angela Stultz-Crawlle is the Director of "S-Corner"… an organization that provides women with education and job training. According to Angela, the training is critical to raising the self-esteem of Jamaican women, many of whom link their value directly to the number of children they have. Verna Foster is a successful "S-Corner" graduate, who is now a construction site supervisor. Verna comes back to the "S-Corner" school to talk to the current students. She tells them "We don't want to make babies… we want to make money… we want to produce, not reproduce".

In San Juan, Pyle chronicles the struggle of a teacher who's truly a living example of the lessons he teaches to his students. Jose Chago Santiago heads up a project to clean up one of the most polluted crime-ridden neighborhoods in San Juan, the Cantera Peninsula. He's getting help from a former student and one-time gang member, Joselyn Rolone. Joselyn counsels kids to stay away from gangs, drugs and violence… and he takes an active role in cleaning up Cantera's pollution problem. Joselyn credits Chago with helping him clean up his own personal life… and says "It's the greatest thing… now people don't fear me… they see me as a catalyst for change."

See video at www.peoplecounttv.com

MAMA CRY
(1996)

Mama Cry (1996)

Boom Boom, Bum Bum ... ... Rataaaa taatta tata ...
silence... sounds of running feet are accompanied by the
crashing sound of zinc fences as persons dash through
to scale the walls behind. Bum Bum ... ratataa. The
sounds of heavy gun fire from the north and south of
the organization's building reverberate throughout the
community and beyond. Many would later tell stories of
their families and friends in distant communities who
shuddered at the deafening sounds. Staff, students and
patients huddle underneath the desks, chairs, clinic
beds, tables, and anywhere they can fit their bodies.
Everyone, irrespective of status and reason for being
there knows instinctively to scurry into hiding. The
hiding places provide only a false sense of security,
however. We are all familiar with the drill, having either
worked in the community long enough or having lived
there long enough to have mastered this survival skill. It
is a lifesaving three step procedure: the DLH.

At the first sound of gunshots, one must Dive (D) to the
floor, Lie (L) flat on your stomach with Head (H) down.

Under no condition should you raise your head. The DLH has become a way of life for many inner-city residents. This particular year, the gang violence and shootings had increased in frequency. The Police Communication Network that reported the national statistics for homicides recorded over a thousand four hundred murders, and our community located in South St. Andrew was one of the infamous contributors. Our community with a population of eleven thousand had recorded an average of sixteen murders per year and countless injuries. Young men in the prime of their lives sat in wheelchairs crippled from the waist down. Being cognizant of this, at the sound of gunshots in close proximity we obeyed like penitent children, only moving when legs and body became too cramped to be ignored.

And so here we are at our place of work, lying on the floor. Each person is straining their ears, trying to distinguish, differentiate and label the types of sounds coming from the streets: fast paced running, panting, light feet, heavy feet, orders of command, more running. From the different sections of the room there is whispered speculation. We whisper in low tones as people do in important meetings and churches. The low whisper forces the other person to reposition their body in an even more awkward and undignified crouch as they strain to hear. No one minds being squashed together; no one objects. It makes us feel safer.

Our hearing and sense of discernment are heightened to those of the blind, and we whisper that like the sounds of the bullets, the running feet are from distinctly different types of shooters. We debate the differences in the sound of gunshots, the size and make of the weapons and who the shooters are. We analyze the shooting strategy, the shots that sound like those coming from heavy machine guns, and the long firing without pause that seems similar to that of the police. We figure that the community's gunmen fire in a short burst then run for cover, then fire, run, stop, fire then run. Someone says, "it sound like the buoy dem, moreover, is only community youths know which section of the zinc fences are weak, so that they can crash through to get to the other side of the road." We surmise that the sound of running feet crashing through zinc fences also means they are being chased. Someone says the running feet sound like the heavy boots that policemen wear and that they heard radio-like sounds. This realization influences the silent ones to join the conversation. From under our sheltered spaces the whispered conversations gather momentum and give way to debate, analysis and conclusion. Unanimously, we conclude the shootings are between the police force and community gunmen!

Eyes widen with fearful apprehension. While none of us is in danger of being directly fired upon, we are caught in the middle. Gunshots have travelled through windows and walls before and do not discriminate. We hear Doctor Lewis groaning in the clinic downstairs, "Me too old fi dis, a nat coming back here, you hear mi, nurse, a not coming back!" No one listens to him. He will be back to tend to the sick on Friday.

After an involuntary gasp at a renewed shooting barrage, "Lawd, Wooh!" the room immediately reverts to silence. And then comes the sound of excited chattering outside, coupled with the distinct sound of a police radio, requesting backup. More heavy feet running to the cry for back up, and shooting resumes. Our conversation stops and we cower even closer, silently praying for the shooting to end.

And then silence that none of us would break. From below on the street a male voice says, "man on the ground, man on ground. A five minutes now me a watch di fucker, an him no git up or move, Yeah mon, dat ded!"

The wailing and screaming coming from the direction of Kidd Lane, three streets north of the clinic, is almost immediate and gut wrenching to hear. A group of women are marching up the road, and in the middle they hold up Miss Olive who is bawling and holding her belly. Occasionally she moves her hand from her belly to push them in an effort to get them to loosen their grip on her. She is a hefty woman and strong; she is determined to make her way to the lifeless body on the ground. Miss Olive has just heard the news: the dead man is her son Everton.

Everton was fifteen, one of five children, the middle child. Miss Olive was a single mother who was employed as a domestic worker to a family in Beverly Hills and also served as the Janitor in an office downtown. She was well known in the community to be a disciplinarian; she disciplined her children through physical beatings that bordered on child abuse. Anything Miss Olive saw near her hand she would use as a tool for beating: the rod of correction, as she described it. She used the dutch pot, *(large circular, usually aluminium cooking* pot) sticks, leather belt, and hose. Any and everything. And, if she were frustrated and tired of the children's truancy and decided it was beating day, every child in the home would be beaten, even if on that day they were well behaved. Miss Olive would remind them of last week's truancy, and that she had been saving up the beating.

It was an open secret that Everton was not like his other siblings. He would get into fights, sleep on the street and Ms. Olive being on the hefty side was never agile enough to catch him for a beating. Daily, the other four children were seen attending school. They greeted the adults they passed with "Good morning" and "Good evening", especially Dean the oldest boy. The contrast in the two boys' mannerisms was the talk in all households. Dean had passed his exams and attended a traditional high school. Soon he would be graduating. Residents even reprimanded him if needed without hesitation. Not so with Everton. No one dared.

The community gossiped about the difference in the children's behavior. Some declared it was genetic. Everton's father was a notorious gunman who was in prison serving a life sentence for multiple murders. The other children had fathers who were bad but not so bad, they said. Ms. Olive's five children were from three different relationships. Some people argued that Everton shared the same father as the two oldest children, and those two had grown into well-behaved adolescents. They pondered, was it because Everton was only a baby when his father went to prison and he never had a father figure or memory of him? Miss Olive's other two baby fathers had shared visiting relationships with their children, but neither provided parental support to Everton.

Other community members were scholarly in their analysis. They related that Ms. Williams, the basic school head mistress, had told them she read in a book that middle children often felt unloved: they were not born in the first batch to be welcomed in the world and they were not the last child to become the favorite, so middle children were overlooked. This reason resonated with many who observed that Everton was a loner; even within his large family Everton was often seen alone. Others disagreed vehemently. They shrugged away the theory in disbelief and provided their own explanation. Everton's bad behavior was because Ms. Olive was always at work, and the boy had too much time by himself without parental supervision; she should quit one of her jobs. Still others simply summarized, "Di buoy jus born fi bad."

On many occasions, residents would observe Miss Olive discreetly making her way to Everton's High School, sometimes heading to the bus stop as if to her workplace before running in the opposite direction to the school. Only recently she had shamefacedly confided that the school had suspended Everton for three days. Despite Ms. Olive's pleading, ranting and threats, Everton refused to resume school after the suspension ended and was now officially a dropout, a corner youth kneading cheap, mashed up weed in his palm. In desperation, Miss Olive turned to the Catholic Church and our organization for help to counsel Everton. However, on the appointment dates, Everton would predictably disappear from home and no one could find him. Soon, neighbors saw him with guns and reported to his mother about his obvious gang recruitment and involvement. Ms. Olive was at a loss about what else to do with her unruly son and was often heard warning him. She would shout. "If you don't stop follow bad company, you gwoine end up dead or in a prison like u dutty puppa!"

Fast forward, and Miss Olive's prophetic words for her son have come true. Everton is now dead, his blood flowing on the asphalt and staining the sidewalk. The smell of blood fills the air. Ms. Olive wails from the depths of her belly at the sadness of not being able to curb him; she wails at the thought that she was not a good mother; she wails for his short life and the fact that her worst nightmare has come true. Despite the signs to the contrary, she also wails for his innocence "Wooooh! wooooh, mi pickney, police kill mi pickney innocently!!! Woooh! Mi pickney mi pickney mi poor innocent pickney!"

The excited crowd gathers and thickens with each passing moment. People push and shove to see the dead body for themselves. There is more bawling and screaming from other family members and residents upon seeing Everton's lifeless body. The scene provokes memories many of them have tried to block, memories of when their own sons and relatives lay dead on the roadside, victims of homicide or police killing. Women, the community mamas and aunties, hold onto each other for support as they bawl. The atmosphere smells of blood and tears.

Stone-faced police with heavy machine guns in hand, stand guard. They corral the area with yellow tape making boundaries and markings of the crime scene. Notwithstanding the shooting exchange between the police and gunmen that the residents had heard that morning, the police face a hostile crowd, which sees them as the face of injustice. They represent a system that has not lived up to its mandate to protect them. It is a system that has often ignored their cry for help in times of fear yet responds with deadly force to maintain social order.

Stories of the morning's chase resulting in Everton's death aggravates an already poor relationship between the police and residents. It is an open secret the JCF and the marginalized poor share a history of mutual mistrust. Jamaica is a stratified, classist society, separating the haves and have-nots by skin shade, class and address location. The police force are a part of the general population and reflect the same prejudices.

In their own defense the police speak of the social ills, high homicide rate, fighting, robberies, and frequent shootings with high powered weapons which happen in inner-city communities. They argue that residents condone violence, withhold valuable information that could lead to arrest and are therefore accessories to crime. Citizens, on the other hand, cite stories they believe justify their distrust of the police: frequent encounters of disrespect, physical and verbal abuse from members of the force, broken trust and corruption they believe to be the main cause of the poor relationship. Many residents provide anecdotes of persons providing the police with information on known murderers and the informants being killed immediately after their disclosure by the said perpetrators. They recount witnessing innocent persons being carted off to jail or being killed by the police. This morning's shooting between police and youth is a familiar scene. Both the police and citizens have each other in stereotypical boxes and treat each other with the associated disdain.

Sirens blazing, police cars speed down the narrow street to provide backup support, forcing residents and meagre dogs to quickly scamper to the sidewalk. The residents hurl insults at the police with descriptive messages of what to do to their mothers, and some throw stones. Amongst the crowd are also onlookers who empathize with the police, but today hypocrisy is necessary for their survival in the community. They too cry along with the crowd, shouting profanity at the police, at times louder than all others. The situation has the potential to escalate and policemen hold their guns tightly positioned across their chests in a way they hope will intimidate and reduce confrontational actions. Overt aggression meets passive aggression, neither side possessing the social training to alter their behavior. As far as the police know, adolescent males have just engaged their colleagues in an intense shootout, and one of the perpetrators now lies dead. As far as they know, one of their colleagues could have been the victim, killed in the line of duty. They too are feeling vulnerable. Exposed, they perceive that every resident is guilty of being an accessory and knows someone who is dangerous. They take no chances.

The sight of heavily armed police walking aimlessly around Everton's body further angers the crowd and sensing this the police nervously fidget with their guns. The crowd is mostly female with a sprinkling of elderly males; the young men have vanished. Inner-city males under the age of 15 and over 65 are perceived to be less threatening and are usually exempt from the hostile encounters their gender experiences with the law and by extension civil society. Inner-city women, mothers and sisters, know only too well the dangers of being a young male in the inner-city. Many families have lost sons to gang war, some being innocent victims of homicide solely because of their gender. In many inner-city communities young males have become an endangered species. The women, mamas, sisters and aunties return home and with determined purpose close their doors, holding their male family members captive inside.

Later in the evening residents will block the main thoroughfare with old car tires and logs making a huge flame in the middle of the street. The yards will be emptied of old fridges and stoves to be placed on each side of the road preventing vehicular movement. Residents will hold up cardboard placards bearing "Justice!" "Murdah." Women and children will cry and lament "we waan justice! Justice, Justice." It is the only time they are given a voice, and the only way they know to attract media attention and to solicit the wider society's sympathy towards their inner-city plight. But, for now, the task is clear: mothers plead and at times become physical to persuade their sons to keep off the street and out of the way of the impending dangers outside their doors.

It is only two o'clock but we close the office and leave for the day. The sight of Everton's body in the street, his mother bawling, tearful mothers re-living their own nightmares, fearful mothers, grim faced looking police, and angry residents, create a roller coaster of emotions. I am saddened by my exaggerated awareness of the social and economic conditions, the volatility of the community in which our organization operates, and the limited resources to make significant, long-lasting change. I am angered by the underlying factors that breed and maintain the cycle of poverty; teenage pregnancy, unemployment, illiteracy, underemployment, hungry and angry youth with guns in their hands. I am frustrated by the international policies that exploit poor countries through unfair trade practices, currency devaluation, high interest loans and the related conditionalities that result in reduced spending for social services like education. I am disgusted by the entrenched legacy of colonial inequities which prevents one class access to resources for transformation, and I am disgusted by the absence of political will to dismantle the garrison inner-city arrangements and inject the necessary capital to transform the communities, stem injustices and improve access to quality education to enable sustainable social and economic mobility.

Our organization tries to fill the gaps, utilizing multifaceted programs: parenting support, health and sanitation, education for school dropouts, and a homework program. The organization's partnerships with churches, private sector organizations and training institutions creates numerous success stories. Some days, we receive unexpected visits from families and graduates whose testimonies of their achievements are so gratifying our hearts are swollen and we are encouraged. But today is not one of those days.

"Enuf is enuff, Miss Angie, too much a we maddas a bawl, every week one a we lose a son, whether from police or gunman; we haffi do something, we want to bring yutes together for peace!" It is a week after the shooting, and the staff and the board chair Horace Levy, a nationally recognized peace advocate, listen attentively while a group of the community's women speak. There are nine women in the room led by Marva, a very dark-skinned woman who is the single mother of five sons including two recognized as notorious gangsters. She has mobilized women from different rival sections: baby mothers, mothers of homicide victims, and active community leaders. Except for Miss Olive who stares listlessly in front of her, the women are passionate in their plea: they are tired of going to funerals to bury loved ones. They quote a chapter from the King James Bible which says that a parent should not bury their child. The mothers with sons already recruited in gangs cry for parenting support, burdened with the fear that their sons would be the next or that they, mothers, would become targets. Unlike their female counterparts who were exempt from violence because of their gender, mothers, and especially baby-mamas, lived with the fear of being a target. We listen as the community women, mamas united and bonded, cry to the only institution they trust for help.

The women had come prepared with convincing arguments that our organization was in an advantageous position to broaden its scope of work to include peace building. With arms gesticulating in front of them and voices at times rising to a high pitch, the women provided stories of how they knew the organization had earned the gangs' respect. They gave as an example the fact that four young male staff members were also residents who lived in opposing sections of the community. These staff members were allowed the freedom to walk across boundaries, secure in the knowledge they were safe and received the same respect shown to all staff. Our intervention programs benefitted the community populace including gang members and their immediate families; we attended to their wounds without prejudice. On staff and among our board directors, we had a cadre of distinguished persons who they argued could appeal to the youths' consciousness. The women had done their homework. Hands which gesticulated earlier now crossed bosoms as they summarized their argument: "Di clinic can do sumpten bout the violence."

Our organization was blessed with a team of persons, experts in specialized areas of development, who also share values of godliness, exhibiting a relationship with a higher being irrespective of our denominational differences. For some of us, counselling was included in our degree programs. But a peace program would call on skills we did not have. The women's calculation of our organization's ability to intervene resonated with us, but we questioned whether we had the capacity.

Not everyone was on board with broadening our work to include a peace program. Yes, they argued, our programs reached all demographic groups. Yes, through our work on the ground we interfaced with gang members on numerous occasions. Yes, gang members had in turn demonstrated their loyalty to us. But did we want to build an even greater relationship with them? A relationship with the gunmen!?

Others reasoned that on the other hand, the gang wars with their unpredictable, frequent shootings affected the lives of all who worked and lived in the community. The fear of being caught in the crossfire affected everyone on many levels: attendance at school, the clinic, sanitation sites and residents' ability to go to their places of employment and to conduct business. And so, our organization accepted the new task and the women's blessings.

Led by Board Chair Horace Levy, we mobilized community leaders: Pastor Carlton Dennis of Bethel Church; primary school Principal Margaret Bolt; the Community Development Committee's President Mr. Irvin Munroe; CDC representatives Mr. Winston Steele and Ionie Smith; other board members; Marlene Campbell, book keeper; and two community women, Miss Monica and the late Marva Brown. The women were selected based on their well-respected, matriarchal status in the community. This group became the first Peace Committee formed to tread on unfamiliar ground. The committee quickly learned that the process to mobilize and coordinate meetings with the two main rival gangs was much easier than convincing them to buy into a peace process. The gangs opposed the idea. Their concept of "peace" was that everyone would stay in their own corners, and not get together in any way. A face-to-face meeting could only be conceived of in terms of every man standing behind a fully loaded gun.

Our first meetings were held with each gang separately: first with the "Response Crew" gang, based at the top of the road, then moving to the opposing "Rat Bat" gang located at the lower section of the community. After that, the Peace Committee had one weekly meeting with each gang. For the first meetings the gang leaders and their "soljas" spoke only of revenge, venting their anger and bottled up hurt. They had all lost close family members, some who were innocent young men gunned down simply because of their affiliation to the corner/ turf the gang occupied. The top gang led by a short light skinned youth named Tulu, blamed Aman, his arch-enemy who led the rival gang, for the bloodletting and for causing the cycle of reprisal killings. These gang members talked of occasions when they had avoided conflict and retaliation in the face of disrespect and open provocation. They painted a picture of themselves as community protectors: defenders of women, ensuring they were not raped, and protectors of residents and homes within their turf from burglary. They all wanted better for themselves and their community and saw themselves as youths who were forced to use the gun for income and protection.

The arguments and reasons for the continued gang feuds and violence were similar on each side. Though not directly political, some of the wars were intricately linked to the relationship that one gang had with political representatives who would often visit that section of the community. As a political garrison community, residents were aligned to and voted along the same political party lines. However, only the bottom gang's Aman, who had a history of fighting in political wars against opposing communities, received the scarce contracts for road repair or for construction work. This encouraged community perceptions of political favoritism.

It took a month of conflict resolution meetings with the two gang leaders and their crews before the now dwindled and fatigued Peace Committee achieved a breakthrough. The gangs were ready to meet each other! But each gang was adamant the meeting should be held on their turf. No one trusted the other or was willing to risk the long walk up or down the street in order to meet. The wall of mistrust had been constructed by layers of tears and fears and it was rock solid. The board chair came up with the only possible solution and every committee member went home to pray for divine intervention. The solution was that every single peace committee member would use his or her body as a human shield and would walk in front of one gang member to the mediation venue on the opposing side. This strategy was based on the knowledge that the gangs would never endanger our lives. In this way our immunity from danger from either side enabled us to protect each gang leader.

The venue was a church located at Brotherton Road, across an open field south of the clinic, where the Rat Bat gang was located. Word spread about our organization's intention and the day for the peace meeting between the gangs became a community affair. In anticipation residents stopped whatever they were doing and lined the streets to see the procession. Sensing and feeling the gangsters fear, women joined us on the walk as closely as they could. This offered more protection. Seven senior gang members went on that walk for peace. As we were about ready to embark, a gang member named Trevor said, "Ms Angie, a can't go wid unnu, sorry." Committee members within earshot risked whiplash as they spun their heads around, bewildered and defeated. This member had gained their respect as someone who sincerely wanted to make changes to his life; he was one of the first to agree and served to motivate his peers to end the tribal war. Now here he was at the ninth hour getting cold feet. Seeing our expressions, he continued, "Miss Angie, I don't have any shoes, I can't go down there in this." He pointed to his shoes. "What if mi dead down there? Mi toes would be sticking out and everybody would come over mi dead body to laugh. Mi need a good shoes."

Without a word, a male staff member took his shoes off and handed them over to Trevor. Without looking back he walked, barefoot, back to our organization's building. A now teary-eyed group re-positioned itself with one gang member between each pair of protectors. Slowly we began to proceed to our destination. It suddenly looked extremely distant. The atmosphere was charged and indescribable; it was noisy yet quiet among us. Within minutes of the start of our walk, more community members, women and men, joined us, creating a tight shelter but also increasing the gang members' vulnerability. Many persons in the crowd blamed them for the emotional trauma they had experienced at some time. Seeing the crowd, Aman, the leader at the bottom, met us halfway. The two leaders shook hands and knocked shoulders. Together we all walked to our destination, the church.

The church was jam packed with excited community and church members. The combination of body heat, nervousness and anxiety made everyone sweat profusely. The situation challenged the committee members' ability to arrange the gangs' seating positions so they could engage each other easily. Outside was chaotic. People had climbed on trees and were standing on tipped toes to peek over shoulders to see inside. The pastor preached, calling on each gangster to turn his life over to God before it was too late to save their souls from impending death, hell fire and brimstone. Neither the committee nor gang members were prepared for the direction in which the meeting was unfolding. A sermon was not what was planned and although it was meant to reinforce an awareness of God and the repercussions for taking lives, the gangs thought being together in the same space would have allowed them to speak with each other rather than listen to a preacher.

Nonetheless, the committee was able to give each leader the chance to tell us how they would proceed in managing conflict differently to maintain peace. The committee was comforted by the rules they developed, but disappointed that the church setting did not allow for the gangs to fully engage each other in a more in-depth way. The first of the rules: "No killing of a man because of a dead man", set the tone for an end to reprisal killings. No raping, no burglary, a fair share of job distribution when there are opportunities, were also among the ten rules. At the end, the community was jubilant with the results, and Bob Marley's "One love, One heart, let's get together and feel alright" blared immediately. The walk back saw gang members accompany their rivals back up the street.

Sometime later, based on this experience our organization received funding to create income-generating programs that could provide alternatives to gang involvement. The two gang leaders encouraged their members to become involved in these activities. One group managed chicken farm projects, while the other group did pig rearing. The proceeds were shared within their respective groups and money revolved within the business and community.

Although some of the gang leaders continued to mistrust the others and stayed within their comfort zones, they did nothing to provoke each other or subvert the process. They too enjoyed the ability to sleep through the night, a luxury not afforded to them when there was gang warfare. Just as the women we had met with earlier hoped, the community's stability also resulted in less police presence and fewer confrontations. The community experienced this peace and stability for the next two years, and no mama cried.

THEY CALLED
HIM BOGLE
(1997)

They Called Him Bogle (1997)

The young man sitting in front of me spoke in the quiet voice of a Jamaican from a middle class or affluent neighborhood. His appearance matched his speech: his neatly pressed, perfectly fitted polo shirt extended just over his waist to cover deep-blue jeans. The pants fitted at the waist, just his size, not baggy or too tight as was the common fashion worn by community youth. Except for a Rolex watch and the gold ring he wore on his middle finger, there was no other jewelry. I concentrated on his face, the light skin, straight features and dark brown eyes that peered directly at me. He held my gaze, watching me as I assessed his appearance and patiently waited for my response. "So, what do you think of my suggestion, Miss Angela?" he asked. I stared at him in awe as I formulated my response. His suggestion of how the organization should proceed under my leadership had floored me.

Bogle, as he was called by community members, had earned the name because of who his character represented.[1] Bogle was an advocate for justice for community youth. His mother had groomed his appearance from a young age. His mastery of the English language was clearly the result of a good upbringing. Bogle neither looked nor sounded anything like a youth from the dreaded Kingston 13 inner-city community. His mother, Miss Dawn, was determined that he would not wear the stereotypical image of the community where he was born, Waltham Park. With the income she earned from her business as the community's dressmaker, she sent Bogle to a prestigious preparatory school outside of the community. As a self-employed person, Miss Dawn enjoyed the flexibility to schedule her working hours to accompany Bogle to and from school by bus in the mornings and afternoons. She survived harsh criticism from her neighbors, especially socially jealous women who behind her back would say, *"She is a wanna-be uptowner; she think she better than we, look pan har to, look how she nose big."* She held her head high and was deaf to the criticisms and the verbal assaults, which at times added to their provocation. These same women would greet her son with, "Good morning Reechoeed!" His given name was Richard, and Bogle could remember his mother's stern instructions not to respond to any other name – *"No pet names, no shortening, no Richeee."* He was Richard, with emphasis on the 'Chard'.

1. Paul Bogle is one of Jamaica's National Heroes. He worked for justice and fair treatment for all the people in Jamaica.

The jeers would eventually end when at the age of twelve Bogle (or Richard) gained a scholarship to an impressive high school. The community erupted in elation and boasted to all and sundry of the boy in their inner-city neighborhood who would be attending one of the coveted high schools on the other side of town. The euphoria was a result of poor people's knowledge of systemic inequity, and the role of education as the most valuable method to cross socio-economic barriers. Bogle's scholarship reinforced their aspiration for their own children to become "somebaddy". Parents knew their children's actualization was intricately tied to their schooling and they knew without a doubt those schools were not located in Kingston 13.

The September following Bogle's news saw two other women in the community registering their children in private schools outside of the Waltham community. The Roman Catholic school within the neighborhood was also forced to erect a huge signpost at their gate informing the public that the fall registration had ended because all spaces were taken. This Catholic school operated a kindergarten and primary school which were more equipped with educational tools than the Government-funded kindergarten, basic and primary schools, and parents were quick to register their children to give them a chance for a better future. The description of Miss Dawn changed from being the 'boasty' woman to one of admiration and respect.

Gang members were also proud of Bogle's achievement to attend a prestigious school and none tried to recruit him. Moreover, they feared the wrath of Miss Dawn who seemed unmindful of their gangster status. Whenever Bogle, in his friendly manner, stopped to speak with them on the corner, she would stand with hands akimbo and feet wide apart scowling at them. Bogle, fearing his mother would embarrass him further, would quickly abandon the conversation and walk towards her. She would then reprimand him loudly for all to hear. *"You hear me, I don't want you to keep company wid dem buoy deh."* She was never intimidated by their reputation and was very vocal on issues that bothered her.

Bogle was an explorer and would traverse the community's lanes and invisible borderlines. His personality and ease with everyone brought him adoration and respect from all, including the gangs. They were proud of him, his education and manner, one of their peers who had gained the education they never had. Bogle developed relationships with all the youths on the different corners and was aligned to none.

With a keen understanding of the underlying causes of social and economic degradation, Bogle soon began teaching gang members to read and write in their own corners. Gang members, even those on our street, did not attend any of our organization's educational programs. They knew only too well the dangers lurking beyond their corners. On a daily basis they faced the possibility of death either by the police or by rival gangs if they crossed the community and this knowledge hindered them from attending our education program. Bogle had gained the unparalleled trust that was only given to one other young man, our U.S. Peace Corps volunteer, Brian Hanley.

Brian was at first trusted because of his status as a foreigner, but he gained the youths' confidence because he would not disclose to anyone their low literacy levels. Many gang members held high positions in their gangs and their egos would not allow them to admit they were illiterate. Brian was a tall, young white male, from the southeast of Washington, DC. He knew how to walk the streets and was comfortable in a multicultural setting. With his non-judgmental approach, adaptability and openness to sharing knowledge, Brian became fluent in Jamaican Patois in short order. Brian was a skillful teacher who incorporated stories of his boyhood years in *"foreign"*, which captured the youths' attention. He demonstrated a genuine passion for social change and soon he became a household name as the community observed his interaction and mentorship.

Brian capitalized on his ability to break new ground and forged relationships with important corporate stakeholders for much needed resources. One such connection was with the movie theatre, the Carib. This partnership gave the chance for local inner-city children and adolescents to go to a movie theatre similar to the ones they saw on their television and have the opportunity to interact with peers outside of their social class. On a given Saturday morning, excited community youth, students and corner youth who had never left the community before were bussed to the theatre. Parents and community members were grateful for Brian's efforts and showed their appreciation through gifts of mangoes and seasonal fruits from their yards. Brian, fully aware they could not afford the gifts they offered, but not wishing to offend, would accept them with his usual grin, "Waaaht, these for meee? Tonks mon, that nice!" He would then share his bundle with the children or yute around him.

Bogle soon partnered with Brian on their corner youth education initiatives. At around two in the afternoon it became a common sight to see Brian going up the road with books and chalk in hand, and Bogle going in the opposite direction, also with books and chalk in hand. Miss Delores, the cook would leave her kitchen duties to stand in the middle of the road, watching them both. And every day she could be heard muttering the same prayer under her breath. "Cover dem, Lord, cover dese brave yute fi me, protect dem Lord, becaz dem is doing ur work. Mmm."

In each section of the community Brian and Bogle tutored, coached and mentored young unattached males. The classes held on both sides grew in student numbers. Teenaged girls boasted of the love letters they received from their boyfriends who attended these classes. Brian and Bogle, two youth themselves, had broken new ground in the area of education. It sealed their identity as mentors. Their actions further motivated the peace enjoyed since the cease-fire between the rival gangs, and community members relished the relative peace.

Bogle's mother was proud of him, of his growth and his ability to access doors of opportunity not otherwise open to inner-city youth. Knowledge of Bogle's education, manner and ability to walk the breadth of the community without fear of attack drew the interest of politicians and building contractors. From time to time, they would request his service to identify and select workers for short-term jobs. They knew his selection would be fair, just and inclusive of all sections of the community. The gangs would also ask Bogle to speak to politicians or others of high repute on their behalf.

Bogle embraced with vigor his appointed position as an advocate on behalf of the community's marginalized youth. His advocacy and demand for just treatment would sometimes lead to confrontations, in which the defiant spirit of his mother rose to the surface and Bogle would refuse to back down. This was essential in his negotiation skills with politicians for community benefit. One such project was the multipurpose sport complex planned by both Bogle and Brian: a basketball court for males and netball court for females. A neutral location was identified and Bogle negotiated with the politician for the land while Brian wrote the proposal and persuaded an established private sector business to construct the courts and signpost. Thereafter the youth had a space for organized, pre-arranged games.

Someone said Bogle's (Richard's) actions epitomized that of Paul Bogle the national hero, and jokingly said, "You should be named Bogle". It was at that moment that Richard became Bogle to the community. The name flowed easily from people's lips, as if he were born with it. Strangely, even his mother who had instructed him never to answer to a pet name, began to call him Bogle. Soon no one could remember the name he had before. He was Bogle.

His question: "So Miss Angie, what do you think of my suggestion, to organize a gun amnesty?" jolted me to back to the present. A gun amnesty! He went on to expand that the idea had come from his intimate relationship with the gang members, some of whom wanted to be involved in alternative income generation activities but lacked the startup capital. Bogle reflected it would be foolhardy to think everyone would be on board with the amnesty as ownership and access to guns was intricately linked to power and underground income. Still, Bogle argued, the time was right, the community was peaceful and this could be the beginning of a movement to encourage youth to give up guns in exchange for investment in income generating projects.

Our organization had embarked on its first peace initiative a year ago, and although it helped to create a level of community peace, some gang members still did not interact, but instead kept to themselves in their own areas and retained their guns. While there was no bloodletting and an agreed peace which helped to stabilize the community, it was not really peace. Residents walked on eggshells as they never knew if or when something would trigger renewed fighting between the gangs. So being well aware of this dynamic, Bogle had a good idea. But he was coming from the grassroots and practical perspective of reducing violence and conflict by simply getting rid of the guns. As an NGO, we knew a gun amnesty would require the buy-in of civil society partners, national security, academics, and different levels of stakeholders. It could even have national implications. Could we undertake this project that could hopefully lead to reform? The first step needed to be setting up a committee of academics to lead the way.

With Bogle's idea, Horace Levy, who was a university lecturer and our board director and Peace Committee leader, agreed to take the first step. He approached the UWI Social Work Department to get other likeminded academics and social advocates like Dr. Barry Chevannes, the dean of the Faculty of Social Sciences, to join with us. The academics, some of whom already knew Bogle from his studies there, were excited to partner with us in a program they believed if successful could be replicated in other inner-city communities. By the following week, we developed a schedule to meet with the different gangs to see if they were willing to meet with us and outsiders, and what factors would encourage them to be part of this amnesty project.

Meeting with the gang leaders was by now not difficult as our organization had already developed a relationship with each gang that enabled them to trust us to be the broker between them and people they had not met before or were unsure of. The logistics for meeting were developed with their input and presented at a meeting held at the university with the academic committee, myself as our organization's director, Bogle and two other community youth. The parameters were simple: the committee would be willing to meet on the gang's turf; no guns would be exhibited; and the academics would introduce themselves by providing their names and addresses. This last requirement evoked consternation among some of the academics who were not comfortable disclosing their address to inner-city youth. Bogle shrugged and in his no-nonsense and quiet voice responded, *"Dialogue of this nature means mutual trust building, let's move on"*.

The first meeting with a gang, albeit with only a few academics, confirmed their willingness to negotiate how they and society would benefit from the amnesty. They agreed to move forward with the discussions as guns for them were a source to economic and social power. The academics committed to developing plans for the committee to take the next step and approach the police and relevant government bodies for amnesty consideration. This was all the result of Bogle, a young man who came up with creative solutions so that the community in which he lived could enjoy another way of life, one that was in peace. And the process had begun.

Bogle and Brian were two young men from two different backgrounds who came together to address the social injustices that they saw. They worked to level the playing field, using peer mentorship, reaching out and becoming role models. Their lifestyle, educational level, and approaches they used filled a gap that staff of the organization could not address.

For Bogle, his mother was a fundamental force in how he evolved; she was vigilant and assertive in guiding him even under the pressures in the community. The importance of this parenting approach should not be underestimated. The school system, with upwards of 40 students in one classroom, created huge challenges. This made strong and supportive parenting even more important.

On Brian's part, as an international volunteer, his easygoing nature and his willingness to share and learn from the community without judgement were essential qualities for his success. As an organization, we learned from these two young men and the community benefitted from their efforts.

The Friday following the first gun amnesty meeting was a day of excitement for youth of the community and those in the adjoining communities. It was the semifinal for the football divisional cup competition. The Bennett Land Football team was competing in the Waltham District Final Football competition in a friendly rivalry with at least ten other neighborhood teams. Winners of the division would then go on to compete in the national game and hopefully win the prize money. Most importantly, they would gain the reputation as the best team in the Southwest Division. The winning of this cup was everyone's dream, on and off the field. Excitement filled the air and young and old could be seen marching up the road in droves, waving their blue and white flags —the color of the Bennet Land football team.

The game began with feelings at a fever pitch, and the spectators watched enthusiastically as youth exhibited a mastery of ball handling skills. The atmosphere was also tense: this was an elimination round, with teams either being eliminated from the competition or advancing to the next level, so the stakes were high. Amid the excitement, snack sellers were out in full force, with an assortment of snacks—peanuts, cold drinks and patties. They made their way through the crowd shouting their wares as they went along. *"Peeeenuttt! Peeenutt! Baaag juice,"* they shouted in the sing-song voice of higglers. Baby mothers and girlfriends wore pleased grins as they watched their men skillfully dodge and evade opponents. Some were not so happy and kept quiet. It was obvious, their man and their team were losing.

Amid the excitement a fight suddenly ensued between spectators on one side of the playground. People were seen scampering away from the scuffle. It was unclear who or what started the fight among the men. Before anyone could intervene, the fight had escalated and the sound of gunshots rang out in rapid succession. Boom! boom, boom, boom! The unexpected yet familiar sound sent panic among spectators and players alike. People ran in all directions bumping into each other and creating a stampede as they frantically ran for safety. Some dived to the ground and were trampled in the rush. When the dust was cleared two youths were on the ground, motionless, dead. One was Bogle. Caught and killed in the line of fire.

The funeral was befitting that of a statesman. Academics, politicians, civil society groups and community organizations all came out to bid their last farewell to a youth that had made us all so proud. Youth from across the community's dividing lines buried their differences and stood solemnly in the pews. The pallbearers were community youths Bogle had taught to read. They tried hard to live up to the expected manly image, not to cry. Still the tears flowed.

There was not a dry eye in the church except for Bogle's mother, Miss Dawn. Miss Dawn's face, though anguished, bore an unfamiliar and indescribable expression as she stood rigidly looking at the casket all the while shaking neighbors' outstretched hands of support.

In contrast to her mother's composure, Bogle's sister Kizzy bawled uncontrollably. Through tears she read the eulogy that her mother had written. In summary, this is what she read:

"I know that many of you here today have heard the story of how my son Richard got his name Bogle. The name Bogle was that of Paul Bogle, our National hero and a freedom fighter. The actions and achievements of my son bear striking resemblance to the man called Bogle. However, I feel compelled to correct you. I, Dawn Stewart, admired the life of Paul Bogle, and so when I was pregnant with my first and only son, I wished him to be fair, just and stand up for others. I am not amazed at how my son lived his life and how he died. He lived up to the name I gave him at birth, Richard Bogle Stewart. He was, and always will be... Bogle!"

KEISHA AND THE CIRCLE OF LIFE

Keisha and the Circle of Life

Her body temperature is over 100 degrees Fahrenheit. Her eyes already appear sunken into the back of her forehead. She is clammy, and I feel compelled to get up again from the bench to beg the nurse's pity. This is a difficult task. On the bench in front of me there are at least twenty angry and frustrated mothers with equally sick babies. Sick babies are everywhere; some have been given a nebulizer for asthma, while nurse attendants administer liquid salts to the children with diarrhea and vomiting. The room has a high scent of Dettol antiseptic, not surprising as the tired looking woman in the blue uniform is dragging along with her an old looking yellow pail and stringy mop, which she uses for a constant, never-ending floor wipe. The two ceiling fans on either side of the room twirl around making a swishing sound. They may as well be turned off, I think, because everyone here is sweating, and profusely too. "Uuugg! Uuugg!" The baby beside me retches in my direction and I scoot down the bench so fast I push the mother beside me, she pushes another, and there's a domino effect. The woman at the end of the bench,

KEISHA AND THE CIRCLE OF LIFE

being knocked almost to the floor with her baby, gets up angrily to demand, "Heeey is what do unnu, eeh?" Her potential tirade is cut short when she sees the baby vomiting on the floor and its mother's helpless expression. Sympathy takes over and she says gently... "maddah, hold har head dong so de vomit doesn't choke har." Then turning her head to the nurses' station, she shouts, "Unnu no see dat de baby dem a dedding here, a dat unnu waiting on to see!"

I am at the Bustamante Children's Hospital, the only children's hospital on the island. I am here with Ameliya my two-year-old grandbaby who had developed a high temperature and diarrhea. Despite my application of grandmothers' remedies and other remedies gleaned from observance at the S-Corner Clinic where I work, the fever had not abated. I had applied the cold-water technique on her forehead and sponged her entire body. When that did not work, I applied the old-style cloth soaked with Bay Rum, wrapped around her forehead. Both remedies were accompanied by heavy prayers. I always get nervous when young babies get ill, especially with diarrhea. The diarrhea came later and I knew the time had come to adhere to Bible instruction. Seek a physician.

The big clock in the center of the casualty department has slowly tick-tocked its way twice around, indicating that we have been at the hospital for over two hours. Yet, we have only moved as far as the diagnostic section. The diagnostic section is the first point of entry in which the nurses assess the urgency of the baby's condition to see the doctor. The place is crammed to capacity even though they have stipulated only one caregiver per child. This means that both parents cannot be in the room at the same time. They just do not have the resources, chairs and space to accommodate us all, so parents and other caregivers must adhere. The security guard standing at the door is a woman of large stature and has a permanent scowl on her face. She has obviously heard all the persuasive stories why two parents are needed to accompany the baby to see the doctor. In robot-like practice, she points to the sign on the door, and repeats her rehearsed chorus, "Mam, I am only doing my work." It was useless appealing for her sympathy and realizing that, parents developed strategies to alternate time spent with the sick baby.

Now it is my turn to be inside the waiting room and every so often I examine my grandbaby, her temperature, her eyes and responses to me. She lies in my arms staring at me or at times appears to sleep - not even a smile can I coax. She is obviously sick but unfortunately does not meet the hospital's emergency criteria. Emergency criteria are saved for accidents, those unable to breathe, and extreme diarrhea. I sigh and use the brochure I found on the ground to fan my face and my grandbaby. Oh lord, I think, poverty is really a *rahtid* crime.

"Miss Angie? Miss Angeeeeie!" exclaims the nurse in the white starched uniform who has just entered the room. "Oh my gosh, Miss Angeeeeie!" Before I can even register her face, the nurse has pulled me and my grandbaby up and is embracing me in a tight hug. She pushes me away from her to scan me up and down, giving me the opportunity to also study her face. At first, I do not recognize her; the face is unfamiliar. Then exuberantly I recognize the smile, the eyes and then the face. She is Keisha. Keisha Mckenzie, the frightened teenage pregnant girl I had met in the inner-city years ago. Now, a nurse? Before I can fully understand what is happening, she is dragging me briskly along with her to the nurse's station. The women on the front bench grumble at her obvious intention and shout in unison. "Favarism, favarism, das why Jamekia cawnt betta, favarism!" To this, she turns around to them and says, "Say what you want, but this is the woman that make me be where I am today. Her school, her Grassroots College saved me. Moreover, me soon come help unnu, alright mi darlings." The grumbling stops, and so does my heart - well almost. It is swollen with pride.

Keisha! Keisha McKenzie is a nurse. I remember her vividly, and suddenly the year 1997 comes flooding back as if it were yesterday.

It was September morning and the first day for the new batch of students entering our second chance education program. Most were dropouts with behavioral challenges and/or learning disabilities, many from broken homes. Some came willingly because of the opportunity it provided; some were forced by parents who waited around through the welcome procedure to ensure their wards stayed in class. Still others were drawn by the promise of a guaranteed daily meal, prepared and served by Miss Olive in the school's canteen.

The morning's agenda included a motivational session, which I facilitated. I could not help being drawn to Keisha. She was a petite teenager with an unusually round face that looked as if she was fighting back tears. From her expression, I could see my talk resonated with her, but surely not enough to cry. I also observed there were times she appeared engrossed in biting her fingernails and lost in a world of her own. I deliberately returned to the classroom in the afternoon. I made small talk with her and questioned what she hoped to achieve in coming to our program. Keisha did not respond and again chewed nervously on her fingernails. I gave her my business card with both my office and personal cell numbers and asked her to call me when she had an answer. She called two days later. Keisha had a secret she wanted to share with me if I promised not to tell her mother. I asked her to come in to see me.

Keisha arrived and I became more curious when once inside my office Keisha asked me to accompany her to the bathroom. With trembling lips she said, "Miss, jus falla me in a de bathroom now. Me waan show you something." Water welled in her eyes and she began to cry but seemed unable to say anything other than "Miss, miss, miss." I convinced her to have another staff member with us. My assistant Marlene, tried to comfort her, but the more she wiped Keisha's eyes the more she cried. The question "what's wrong?" was met with more tears and loud sobbing. It was obvious the answer depended on going to the bathroom. The bathroom was small and we squeezed in. Keisha lifted her blouse which exposed a black spandex girdle. She began to undress, first taking off the girdle. Silent with mouths wide open we watched as Keisha tediously unveiled layers of tight spandex from around her waistline. With each removal, her belly protruded further to finally expose a ballooned pregnancy! Freed from its bondage, the fetus jumped in a dancelike move in her stomach. We literally had to use our hands to close our mouths. We were dumbstruck. How had she concealed this belly to such an advanced stage of pregnancy?

Keisha was five months pregnant and through hiccups whispered, "Could we arrange with the clinic help to have an abortion?" It was not that she feared gossip or did not know who was the baby's father, or that her mother would throw her out and she would be homeless, but rather her request came because of the feeling that she had let her mother down. Her two older sisters had become pregnant teenagers and now crammed their children into the small two-bedroom home the family occupied. Keisha cried that she had vowed to herself and her mother she would never become part of the community's statistics for teenage pregnancy. She would graduate with matriculating subjects that could take her into an accredited vocational center. She would become somebody, make her mother proud. Yet here she was in the same predicament as her sisters and so many other young girls.

Her mother, Miss Yvonne, was a member of S-Corner's female co-operative group who managed a chicken farm and benefitted from the additional income. She was a single parent and mother of five. With great unease we called her to the office. Miss Yvonne was clearly uncomfortable and refused the seat we offered her. She was further agitated when she heard sobbing in the adjoining office and recognized Keisha's voice. I will never forget the look of defeat as she looked first at me and then at Marlene. With full comprehension of the situation, Ms. Yvonne sat down. She was beside herself with the sadness of lost dreams. She wrung her hands and paced the office mumbling more to herself than to us. "Mmm, why me leave Mocho, mmm why mi leave?" She lamented that she should have left the community and returned to the hills of St. Elizabeth which years before she had run from in search of a better life in Kingston. "Or", she muttered, "Mi shoulda did send dem to live with them great grandmadda."

There was no teenage pregnancy in her lush village, Mocho, and gunshots could be heard only on the television. But Miss Yvonne, despite the challenges of raising four girls in an inner-city community could not bear the separation from her children. She lamented further that she did not know her father, and her mother had migrated to England leaving her with her grandmother and the promise of her return. Her mother never did return, and the parcels and boxes she sent gradually ebbed as her mother created her new family "a foreign". The experience of not growing up with her parents and her yearning for those bonds resulted in Ms. Yvonne's pledge never to separate from her children.

When Keisha's baby was born, S-Corner donated a customized cot for the baby. Our organization networked with individuals, both local and overseas, who would make periodic donations of second-hand clothing, books and goods. Many community parents and students benefitted with shoes and clothes, which enabled them to attend their various schools. In our efforts to encourage baby mothers to attend our second opportunity school and reduce the attrition rate, the teachers also allowed for time off during the school day for new mothers to return home to breastfeed. Keisha was able to utilize this support and she attained the required grade average in all subjects. She graduated from our educational program, the Grass Roots College.[2]

Keisha was among five female recipients of S-Corner's Second Opportunity Program who went on to practical nursing school that year. The S-Corner Second Opportunity Program was an extension of our regular

---

2. In addition to the Grassroots College, S-Corner provides scholarships for vocational skills training programs.

education program, and provided the graduates with financial support to pursue vocational skills from recognized, accredited institutions. While some students had to pursue menial and short-term jobs because of their immediate and dire needs, each year the majority of students pursued diverse vocational training courses to enhance their ability to compete in the main stream employment realm.

Back at the hospital, it's now 2015 and I am trying to keep up with this brisk walking nurse holding my hand. Keisha takes me straight inside the hospital's treatment room and gently relieves me of my grandbaby. She questions where the mother of the child is and takes a yellow pass from her pocket. She scribbles on it and instructs me to show the scowling security guard at the door. The pass allows two parents to be inside the room. Keisha takes charge of the situation and in quick succession both mother and I are inside the doctor's office. We are treated as very privileged persons and my grandbaby receives the medical attention she needs. Her temperature reduces and with the prescribed medication she bounces back to health.

Divine intervention or karma? I shout blessings to the homes of our donors who by their generous support of our educational program had transformed lives and created generational change.

Two days after I left Keisha at the Bustamante Hospital for Children I called her and she described her journey:

Miss Angie, my daughter is now 18 years of age and going college. To be honest a don't think if I was still living down S-Corner Lane she would be going college and I never want har to end up like me, caz it was sooo hard. I wanted to stay and help give back to the community, the organization that do so much for me, but a couldn't stay and take the risk wid my daughter. I had to run. Many days me go bed hungry to make sure she eat and go school. I wanted to send har to school where pickney not fighting in a class every day and the teacher cant bother, and she can come home and sleep on her bed not under it becaz gunshot a fire. I am married now wid two other children so in all I have three children.

When I graduate from nursing school I went to work in several nursing homes before getting the job here at children's Hospital. Working here for a government hospital I earn less than what a use to get, but they withdraw tax and contribution to the National Housing Trust. Working here I can also borrow money and send back myself to Nursing school. It took years of paying back and sacrifices but we did it.

A meet mi husband in the church and we pool together we partner draw savings, and with the eligibility points from the National Housing Trust (which provides low interest mortgage), we buy a lickle house in Portmore. Mama live wid us.

The Portmore community is a lower middle-income community outside Kingston, yet it constitutes a significant leap from the shantytown section of the

Waltham Kingston 13 area where she had lived. The detached housing scheme also provides land space for building expansion. Keisha had done what she knew in her heart she always would do. Through donors like Jamaican Self-Help Canada and Christian Aid UK who funded our educational programs, the S-Corner Community Development Organization's multi-faceted efforts had indeed transformed this life.

Images of
Righteousness
(1999)

Images of Righteousness (1999)

It is Monday morning, 9 o'clock, and St. Joseph's Road located off the Waltham Park main road, is bustling. Women with anxious faces tightly grasp the hands of small children who appear reluctant to walk. The women walk briskly forcing their young wards to quicken their pace to a trotting rhythm, while clusters of older looking children break into a run at the sound of the nearby school bell. Along the road, groups of people: men, women, children and youths, huddle in animated conversations. From the rapid arm swaying and the astonished expressions on their faces, it is clear something exciting has just occurred. I continue down the narrow road driving slowly to manage the frequent bumps on cement patched potholes.

In the Waltham low-income community, residents live in tenement yards. Although families in a yard may not be related, they share social amenities: toilets, kitchen, and "illegal" utility connections. Where politics, safety and security are concerned, people tend to group themselves on the basis of social trust. This morning groups have formed by gender, age, and church affiliation. On hearing the approaching vehicle, some persons look up, recognize me and the car, and excitedly shout something to me. The words are indistinct and I am unable to understand what they are saying. The morning is noisy; the happy chatter of school children playing has not abated with the sound of the bell that echoes over the concrete wall of St. Peter Claver Primary School and merges with the sound of traffic from the busy Waltham Park thoroughfare.

Sitting directly in front of the school gate, five female vendors display trays laden with a wide array of sweets. Sweets of different colors, assorted shapes and sizes lure the more than six hundred school children to their trays. I had often thought that the one community dentist located on the main road should pay these women commission fees for their guaranteed clientele.

As if on an invisible cue only they could see, the women simultaneously wave to me. I acknowledge their greetings and wave back. It's good to work in a community where everyone knows your name and who you are, especially in a community ravaged by internecine violence.

The atmosphere is reminiscent of a Friday evening; the only things missing are the pots of soup on the sidewalk and the jerk man preparing chicken. Yes, this has to be a day-time identity crisis, Monday morning masquerading as Friday evening!

The aura of excitement permeates the air. I try to concentrate on the task of driving. Driving in any of Kingston's inner-cities usually fills one with trepidation, as a single unavoidable mistake has the potential to become every driver's nightmare: you hit someone and you encounter intense wrath and have to be rescued in time. If not, you had better possess the God-given ability to outrun Usain Bolt! Simply put, there is no room for apology, discussion or even explanation. The circumstances that cause you to hit one of their own, especially a child, are irrelevant. They think not of the toddlers walking out of their yards onto the busy streets in search of their mothers, nor the youth riding bicycles out of a side alley onto an oncoming vehicle's path, testing the involuntary reflex of the driver. They dare you to hit them, while you maneuver your vehicle from and between mongrel dogs lying across the street too hungry to move. They too know they are untouchable. It's their territory, their birthright to the streets. Maybe my status as the director of the community health center, dedicated peacemaker, Rasta "empress", and social intervention specialist would have altered my fate if such bad luck ever befell me. I do not know. I pray I never have to find out.

Youths are lounging relaxed on the corner—no peeping from behind rusty zinc fences! They stand in groups talking among themselves. I recognize most of them, the usual corner youth, lookout soldiers, the hand-middle kneader mashing his marijuana into fine powder to create the perfectly shaped spliff which he would light any second now. The gun-bag boys are also out, and so too are the night owls, the real Night Owls! I do a double take. Night Owls? In the broad daylight? Something is different about this Monday morning. I cannot ignore the inclination to stop; the intuition, gut feeling to really listen, ask, someone, anyone. Deliberately I slow the car almost to a halt as a strategy to encourage someone to again shout clearly to me the message persons have been shouting as I pass them by. I need to, I absolutely must hear clearly what they are shouting. Working in the inner city, survival depends on acute situational awareness, street wisdom, and the ability to make quick decisions–fight or flight.

The night owls are watching me. They nod and lift their hands in salutation. Night owls do not smile; they hold high positions in the gang hierarchy and exemplify militancy. These are the informal protectors, turf soldiers who protect the community from rival gangs. Nighttime sleep is a luxury they cannot afford so they sleep during the day. Night owls welcome the dawn of the day; it is the only time they allow themselves to embrace sleep, close their eyes even for a while. They trust no one, no environment or situation. Sunrise, the light of dawn, children going to school, the hustle and bustle of employees going to work and the shop keepers opening businesses, create an atmosphere of normalcy and sense of safety.

Gang leaders and rank-and-file members trained to expect the unpredictable have implemented rigid systems for their safety. Corner "yutes" with innocent faces provide lookout services and have mastered the uncanny art of alerting their lieutenants to danger without moving an inch from their assigned post. These corner youths know only too well the seriousness of these assigned positions for their own safety and the safety of their families. They are lookout soldiers; they have no weapon; they are alert, discerning, and cannot be distracted or wander from their post. The alarm signal must be sent at the first sight of danger or even the perception of danger. Danger comes in two distinct forms that share important characteristics: one is the State, with legal authority to shoot based on the perception or reality of a dangerous situation; the other, the rival gang with the order to kill all male youths living in the territory of a rival gang. Both are armed and extremely dangerous.

As I slowly drive down the road I can at last distinctly hear Dimple's voice shouting, "Miss Angie, Peace! Peace! A peace time!"

It's Monday March 16, after Friday the 13th. Oh my gosh, yes, it's peace! It has to be. What other circumstances could explain the night owls giving up their well needed sleep to be out in the day? The notorious Tulu and Shaba are standing among the bustle in front of the school gate. I am tempted to stop as I am eager for news, an update, on what had changed over the weekend.

Memories of just last Friday engulf me. The staff of the community health center had hurriedly packed our bags and fled. We had received two direct and similar messages from the rival gangs: at about 10 am Friday morning, the Rat Bat gang's don Aman had sent his solja, "Miss Angie, we need you to close the clinic because we don't want you in the cross fire." Aman was a veteran, the oldest living don. He was around 40 years of age and had ruled his turf for over twenty of those years. He was a small man, thin in stature with beady eyes and straight nose set in an oval shaped face. He was always well dressed and could easily pass for a racehorse jockey. He had strong political ties, was notorious, and his enemies feared him. He was also cautious, always walking with his gun on his hip cowboy style and fearing no one except his wife Sonia. The community gossiped of her gun-butting him and punching him unconscious when she believed he was cheating. Rumors once circulated that he shot one of his lieutenants in the foot for gossiping about his domestic abuse situation.

Shaba, the Response Crew don sent a similar message. "Miss Angie, a need you to leave now because mi nuh want notting to happen to you or your staff." Shaba was the darkest shade of black, with high cheekbones, and eyes semi-closed as if he had just smoked the best weed on the island. He was thick and muscled with not an ounce of fat. He had explained to me his addiction to physical exercise while imprisoned, being bored and unable to read. He was a calculating thinker and revengeful. His enemies fantasized about killing him. His serious demeanor made strangers wary of him and his enemies cower.

The office was located in the middle of the community with windows overlooking both ends of the road. Staff members had peeked through the office windows on both sides and were already grabbing their bags and fastening windows in preparation to leave. Outside, youths armed with Uzis, Glocks and M-16s in hand stood behind light posts, behind their zinc fences, silently waiting for us to leave. Somebody was going to die that night.

That Friday morning began as one of those weird days when you woke up from a good night's rest, yet the events of the day progressively worsened. By noon you knew you should have slept in, covered your head with the nearest blanket and postponed getting up. I didn't; I had gotten up and this was how the day went.

"Empress, cover your locks before you can speak to me!" she spat loudly for all to hear. The words came from the Rastafarian woman I had stopped to offer a ride. Her rebuke was searingly painful. Around the crowded bus stop on-lookers stopped whatever they were doing, conversation ceased, and everyone looked on with anticipation. The atmosphere was tense, silence only broken by the sound of early morning cars zipping past. A middle-aged woman standing by with two small children eagerly searched my face for a response, and a schoolgirl looked amusedly at me, all the while chewing furiously on a piece of gum, blowing bubbles and making popping sounds.

The crowd waited, holding their breath for the verbal cuss out they were sure would result from this loud reprimand. This scenario was rare, unique and, chances were, unlikely to be repeated. No, this was not a common marketplace scene; it was not often the public would witness two Rastafarian women, two empresses, clash. I glanced at myself in the rear-view mirror and wondered again for the tenth time in the last few seconds, why I had stopped to give this 'holier than thou' empress a lift in my car. The answer was obvious to even the bubble gum blowing teenager: she was Rastafarian, a "sister".

We, more than any other religious group in Jamaica, experience discrimination daily; a history of persecution, subtle messages which were sometimes not so subtle. Our advocacy against neo-colonialism and an oppressive system created tension between Rastafarians and successive governments. In the early 1960s, the then Prime Minister, Sir Alexander Bustamante directed the Jamaica Constabulary Force to "round up all Rastafarians and trim them". Rastafarians were beaten, shorn and killed. Songs were written about us and sung with great gusto; jeering songs describing our way of life and our nappy hairstyle. Rastafarian children were not accepted in schools. Institutional policies dictated all students be groomed, hair cut short and combed. In accordance with our Nazarene vows, Rastafarians' hair is never cut and remains uncombed. We were called "dreads", short for dreadful looking. We were said to have forty legs (an insect) crawling on our heads; we ate food without salt and were malnourished. The propaganda list was long.

Motivated by our shared religious ideologies and assumed shared experiences I could see this sister was obviously in need of a lift. She carried heavily laden bags in both hands; bags competing to see which would drag her hands further to the ground. Whoever had packed those bags had packed them well. The bags bulged at the sides and peeking out of the top of one bag was a brown dry coconut. Standing beside her in proud upright positions were the brooms; the symbolic marking of the Bobo shanti Rastafarians. The empress was obviously going to need a very understanding minibus driver to accept her with her bags and brooms.

Her loud and angry repetition of, "Empress go cover yourself before you can talk to me," jolted me out of my reverie and I now focused on her face. Even though angry, the sister was beautiful. If you could see beyond the heavy scowl that knitted her forehead, her lips curled angrily showing even white teeth. She had big eyes set wide apart, an Ethiopian looking nose and an oval shaped face. Her red turban was wrapped high above, beginning from her forehead and shaped like a pyramid; only many years of locks could maintain that height. Her long yellow dress flowing all the way to her ankles was tied at the waist with a red, green and gold band, with long sleeves covering her arms, reminding me of Mary Poppins. This sister, although apparently young in age, was no princess; she was an Empress, an elder in her own right!

As a Rastafarian myself, I easily identified her as a Bobo Shanti Empress. These sisters, like the Nyabinghi sisters, are strict in their adherence to our religious belief. This belief is manifested in our way of life, as the old testament assigned gender roles for females including our dress code and social interaction. Rastafarian females are subjected to society's stereotypical gender role, and more so by the religious ideology that females were created from the rib of the male. As such Rastafarian women are treated as subordinates. These sisters are generally accepting of their subordinate position. Unfortunately, and quite frequently, one glance at me would provoke these otherwise quiet sisters into uncontrollable wrath. Only today, I was not in the mood for the preaching and judgment. Ego would not let me. Intelligence, common sense, and ego fought.

Intelligence reasoned, "Do not give the public something to smirk about. You are both empresses: she is a traditional sister, you are more liberal. And just look at you through her eyes. Uncovered locks blowing in utter defiance and dressed in corporate attire." I knew she, along with the onlookers, could not see my full clothing, but what they could see would feed their imagination about the rest. Moreover, they would embellish the story tonight when they relayed it to their families. Common sense taunted, "A good, you know those sisters see you as "society Rasta" that don't know Jah, so you should a leave her."

In the end, logic and intelligence shied away from the confrontation, two against one. But, ego, lord help me, too late! Shame now joined ego. Ego won hands down! I was tired of being judged and placed in a box for my appearance. The sister had to know that. With gritted teeth, I responded, "Sister, you need to go read your bible again, because if you had any discerning power you woulda recognize me as the angel that Jah sent to carry you, and u bag an pans. Now fuck off!" And for good measure, I shouted, "Anybody waant a ride, just hop in a dis!"

Driving off in a cloud of dust, ego intact, I reflected on the scenario with shameful sadness. I was feeling sad, tired and emotionally drained. It was not the sister's fault how she perceived me. She was just different in her religious interpretations and expectations of another Rastafarian sister. I should have been more tolerant. But earlier in the morning a similar scene had played out with my husband. The reason for the fight? My dress code. My husband, a Nyabinghi Rasta man, did not believe my image was that of an empress, a righteous woman. Worse, one who had a king! My way of dressing embarrassed him. He detested my business attire and compared me daily to my two best friends, Empress Myrna and Empress Imani who were always decked out in outfits depicting African pride. They even had matching head wraps. I wore suits or solid colors in mostly earth tones or black and white. My skirts though long were slit to the thigh and to make matters worse, they were close fitting. I loved my dress code and was adamant that my relationship with God; my being, my life's work and purpose were what counted in the pursuit of Godliness. However, my image seemed to be in extreme contrast to the neatly designed box they had constructed for me.

The Friday morning's encounter between me and the empress, reminiscent of so many other fights with Rastafarians, made me now ponder. Were they right? Was my husband right? Should I pay more attention to my image, conform to society's stereotype of Rasta women, wear more African clothes, wrap my head to cover my locks, wear long loose skirts and blouses that covered my arms and ankles? An image of righteousness? The image of me dressed like a penitent Bobo Shanti empress made me shudder. I glanced quickly in the rear-view mirror as if to reassure myself I did not look so out of the box, so Babylonian, so Jezebel, as my husband described me. Oh Lord, wrong move. I should not have looked because now I could see myself through their eyes: heavily applied mascara eyes on already long lashes made them look utterly fake. To make it worse I now noticed a button had come loose providing a peek that showed my chain with a trademark Ethiopian Orthodox cross nestled between my breasts. Oh dear!

Today the criticisms had infiltrated my being, my consciousness. For the first time in my fifteen years as a Rastafarian I questioned my identity. Who was I? Mainstream society, oblivious of the nuances of how we as Rastafarians worship, identified and related to me according to their perception of Rastafarians. My locks were too lumped together, too unruly, too long and unkempt for me to be treated any differently. To the mainstream public I was not a conscious African sister who chose to wear sister-locks as a demonstration of naturalness, while at the same time making painstaking efforts to erase all natural nappiness with so-called "natural" oils and gels. No, mainstream society looked at my lumped uneven locks and treated me with the same intolerance they showed to all Rastas—whenever I walked into corporate offices for appointments or service I was usually the last to be served. I was often patronized; false smiles people thought were convincingly welcoming. Their faces were paintings of contradiction: smiles drawn back while eyes reflected disdain.

With the knowledge of who I am, I look to Rastafarians for acceptance, to see in their eyes recognition of who I am. I am a daughter of Zion, a woman of God. Yet, they too look at me through eyes of judgment, eyes of rebuke, eyes that have taken their Nazarene vows seriously, which include how a woman should present herself. My dressing is too sensual, stylish, conflicting with the stereotypical image of the Rastafarian female. Never mind that my work, my deliberately chosen career to manage a social work agency in underprivileged communities aligns with my religious beliefs and life purpose. I work in communities where many Christians and Rastafarians have feared to tread, facilitating change among the vulnerable marginalized poor, to teach and coach there. I work to build individual and collective capacity to improve living conditions through social and economic interventions, mixed with heavy doses of praying, respecting their religious ideology, moral values and spirituality. Yet, in the process, Christians pray I find God as I pass them by.

Uncertainty filled me. Maybe they were all right. Should faith and dress be mutually exclusive? Can they not coexist in the same person? Maybe I needed to re-examine how I presented my image. It is not passive or reverent enough. It is also definitely not African. I had heard of a good dressmaker who sews nice long dresses, skirts and long sleeve blouses. I decided, this weekend I should visit her, armed with material to make some nice long dresses and head ties to match. My mascara would also be dumped. Time to fit myself into that religious box. Time to gain acceptance from my own. I am tired of being judged. No more "fire bun!" would be chanted on this sister.

I was deep in these thoughts when I arrived at my workplace on the Friday morning. The top of the road was empty; no one, not even the usual corner youth. And yet, I could feel many eyes on me. Eyes from behind rusty zinc fences, eyes from behind walls, eyes everywhere. Three meagre dogs lay on the ground, defiant, not moving. Chances were they had already rummaged the pile of garbage on the sidewalk only to find washed out tin mackerel or sardine cans, along with chicken bones chewed to a mince by hungry humans, not worthy of a scavenger's efforts. I slowed to the required stop awaiting the predictable voice of the owner, usually a woman, to shoo them out of the road. The dogs pattern their owners' habitual lifestyle; the roads are their verandah. Young women would also sit on the side of the road gambling, feet spread out into the road, while children and babies walked across to the nearest shop or neighbor's yard oblivious of the dangers.

Yet on this Friday morning there was no one to shoo the dogs... just an eerie empty street. I glanced upwards, and my eyes locked with a youth's. He was kotched between the trunk of the big Tamarin tree, Uzi in hand. Ready. I knew him, he knew me. He greeted me with a nod. A thousand words conveyed though nothing was voiced, just understood. Oh, when had we come to this?

A month before the community stability had been broken by a rapid spate of reprisal killings that reached an unprecedented level. We now had six homicides and numerous injuries in one small community. Among them was Typan, a wind screen wiper, a youth everyone knew was not involved. He had been shot in the stomach and clutching his belly he had staggered and stumbled up the road towards the clinic before he collapsed in front of the office. Before I even had time to think, Dian, a staff member was handing me my car keys with orders to "drive Miss Angie Drive!" Strong women had bundled Typan into the back seat of my car, sandwiched between my office assistant Marlene and another woman. A young woman jumped in the front of the car with me and sat on the window, her entire body hanging precariously outside while she screamed at pedestrians, "Move!! Move, ooono move out a de waay!" With hazard lights blinking, we sped ambulance-like down Spanish Town Road, onto Darling Street before reaching the Kingston Public Hospital. Trained porters met us on arrival and wheeled him away, with Marlene running behind them to say, "Save him Dacta, save him, a one innocent yute!" Around us people were gasping at us and I looked down to see my blood-soaked clothes. It was the first time I had ever fainted.

As an organization that operates in the middle of an inner city, we are forced to address issues of peace and community stability on an ongoing basis. With this shooting, our previous peace effort was now broken. Our organization's ability to implement social development programs was severely affected; classrooms were empty, the clinic had dwindling numbers of patients, and streets were mostly empty. The public pressure on the police force mounted and soon they were forced to justify their pay with sound intelligence. Corner youths not involved were carted off to jail and beaten for information, and there were deadly confrontations between police and gun men. Peace is a necessary precursor for social, economic and environmental development and our organization struggled along with other resident community-based organizations to alleviate these situations. But when there is access to guns, just one incident leads to a roller coaster of reprisal killings and the fragile peace is broken. Peace is gone and with it lives are lost.

The biggest challenge to community development is peace building. Gun access is a much broader issue that moves beyond our community to the wider Jamaican society. While we continue to offer programs at the community level for local youth, women and others, there has to be effective nation-wide efforts, policy development and innovative informed actions, to stem the tide of guns coming into the country before they reach the hands of youth who are mostly illiterate and struggling in impoverished communities. Jamaica does not make guns, so ports of entry must be sealed. A national consensus and strategy informed by civil society organizations and those working on the front lines must be in place for efforts at the community level to be truly successful and sustained.

When on that fateful Friday the messages came from both sides of the gangs for us to close the office and leave, I mused. "Ok, what else could go wrong?" It seemed to be my day for taking orders. First it was my husband's demand for me to change my dress to appear more virtuously Rasta, then the holier than thou empress' demand that I cover my locks, and now these two messages from gangsters demanding our staff leave. Oh, what a Friday it had turned out to be!

I looked through the window and I saw Shaba directing his men to take up strategic positions. An apprehensive and weary staff informed the board directors of the situation. We were all tired, emotionally and physically. Our morale was deeply affected and we discussed the implications of running, and if we could leverage their need for our programs. Acting on the advice of the chair, Horace, we sent the gangs word of our position. If we left today based on their orders, we would close the organization's door forever. It was a huge gamble, but one we were prepared to make. There was no response.

As we prepared to leave I had a compelling urge to take off my pendant, my Ethiopian Cross and give it to one of the dons. I was unable to provide a rational explanation for why I would give my chain and Ethiopian cross pendant to a gang leader. It went against the tenets of operating in an unbiased way. All of us understood that the organization, and I as leader/ manager, should never be perceived as taking sides. My safety and the safety of the organization weighed heavily on every action; being non-biased must never be compromised.

Yet, I was very conscious of a presence, the presence of God who inspired my action, really, commanded me to give my chain as a last effort to Shaba who I had just seen. I was confused, weak and I needed to be alone. I stayed back to pray after the staff had left. This time I made a customized head wrap, using a sheet from the clinic to cover my head. I covered my locks and got down on my knees in total surrender. The command was clear, and I obeyed. It was indeed the day to take orders. I prayed for peace and protection and handed over the cross to one of the youth I saw on my way out, with the simple instruction, "Give this to Shaba, he will understand." That was Friday afternoon.

Now it's Monday morning and all is calm. What had happened over the weekend to bring about this unpredictable 180-degree shift in the community? From staff fleeing from the community in its heights of preparation for indefinite war… to peace! We learned from the bits and pieces of the stories that after the staff had left there was a standoff between the two gangs. Both gangs stayed on their sides of the invisible boundaries; no one moved, not a single shot was fired. Both sides were heavily armed, prepared. Yet, each side waited on the other to make the first move. The same thing occurred the following day, Saturday. Just an icy, tense calm. People stayed in their houses for fear of being caught in the crossfire; children were kept inside and watched television all day. They ventured outside only to go to their outside toilets; voluntary prisoners in their homes, peeping and listening.

The residents recounted that at about 12 noon on Saturday, they saw Shaba, white handkerchief tied on his head, no shirt on and with hands held high in the air. He walked down the road in the direction of the rival gang, to meet with Aman. The gang's solja saw him and aimed, but Aman shouted, "No man fires a shot" and stopped everyone in their tracks. The residents said Aman laughed loudly in disbelief and amazement and said to Shaba, "Man u brave no rawse claawt, u know!" Shaba kept his hands up, then the men fist bumped and did a man bounce on each other's shoulder. The soljas looked on in bewildered amazement and nervousness, not sure what to do as the two dons talked. And then Shaba and Aman spoke, "War done, man and man a go live in peace!"

I can now understand the Monday morning's fever of excitement. It is contagious and I have caught a full dose. But more than anything I need to hear from Shaba himself what had influenced him to make such a daring move that could have cost him his life. I need to also hear from Aman in his own words why he had stopped his men from shooting and fulfilling their fantasy of killing Shaba.

Shaba explains, "Miss Angie, when a see you and you staff drive off, cutting short u work to help people, so we could a kill each other, a say no sah. No Lord, no. Then a see Bowla bring me something in his hand and tell mi the clinic plan to close for good, I feel bad. Then I look and see that is your chain, your cross. I can't tell you the feeling whey come over me. Me had to go sit down, mi couldn't move. So, I just put out more soldier to watch, but a call off the mission to attack. A tell dem mek we wait fi dem to come up, we naw go down. The next morning a take up the chain, and I take up the gun... Miss Angie, me have mi "Johnny" over three years now, mi know how it feel, that day it was soo heavy mi couldn't lift it up much less to fire! So, a put it down and keep trying, but a notice as long as I have the chain in my left hand, the gun in my right feel well heavy. So, I put the chain one side and take up the gun and everything was good again. By this time, I feel to test the chain further so I put it on my neck, and Miss Angie, a could not lift the gun! So, I know what I had to do, it had to be one or the other. Somehow me know seh once I have on my chain them cyan do mi nothing either. I did just feel like I am protected by the Most High! God a God! So, I surrender! No more war. Peace, A God mi seh! Dem seh Jesus forgive seventy time seven, me is not Jesus but we can learn!"

Aman is grinning at me showing off dazzling gold front teeth. He says simply, "Miss Angie, we get the clinic message you kno, we respeck ur organization an we don't waan be the one fe stop it. We no want be de one to start a war, so we a wait... Me never shoot a man yet wid him hands up in the air. Me want hear what him haffi say first.... and when de man Shaba greet me and say Peacee... Me haffi say Peace, cause man don't haffi war, we can talk."

The tears flow. They are tears of joy and affirmation of God's divine power. I feel like shouting. Yes Jah! Yes God! Almighty Yahweh/Jehovah, miracle worker, thank you. I give thanks for our organization's ability to leverage our power as an agency of change. I pray for stronger faith to serve him, to continue the work that I do. I pray that even when in doubt of my identity—am I Rasta enough, am I Christ-like enough, and am I dressed as others dictate the image of righteousness to be, I will be confident that my relationship with God is so much bigger than their religious boxes, peculiarities and differences. I pray for those who do not accept me as a woman of God, a daughter of Zion. I know when it's time to worship, I will cover my head, I will dress as the Sarah that I am. Other times I will fly my locks as free as a bird, proud of my relationship with the creator and knowledge of my purpose. It is who I am and all that I am. A woman of God! Selah.

His Name Was Sheldon

SIGNS AND WONDERS

His Name Was Sheldon

Zz, zzzzz, my cellphone whirred before the familiar ringtone belted out *"If Jah is standing by my side"*. I sang along with the artist, "Tony Rebel" in my off-key way deliberately letting the phone ring until the second verse, *"Then why should I be afraid"*, before I answered. It was Sheldon, an ambitious community youth and a recent graduate of our educational program. He reminded me in his patient voice that he was waiting for me in front of the centre's building. I had forgotten that I had promised to give him bus fare for work. I assured him I was on my way. "Please don't leave", I said, "I am just ten minutes away."

Mmm, ten minutes would be more like twenty in the heavy morning traffic. I chided myself for not writing this appointment in my diary. Had I remembered, I would not have stopped at the "jelly man" at Heroes Circle for my ritual coconut water. It wasn't like I was thirsty; it was just a habit I enjoyed. Each day I would stop by the jelly man and chit-chat while he chopped the coconut to a thin layer before handing it to me. I enjoyed

155

putting it to my lips for a guzzle. Much to the embarrassment of my three girlfriends, Empress Myrna, Lorna and Carol, I refused to accept the straw that coconut sellers now offered to females. They thought me uncouth and would literally turn their backs while I put the large coconut to my mouth and drank from the top of it, not putting it down until I had consumed all the water. This was the traditional way Jamaicans drank coconut water and I saw no reason to change this practice. For good measure, I would let out a loud belch, further embarrassing my sister-friends. They denied me as Peter denied Jesus.

Thoughts of Sheldon made me smile. Sheldon, ah, determined ambitious Sheldon. He had won my heart and that of his teachers and all who came in contact with him. Sheldon was eighteen, tall and lanky from self-imposed starvation and had a pleasant easy-going personality. He was the only male in his family of six. Sheldon had confessed to us his concern for his mother Sandra, who worked as a domestic worker doing 'day work' to support him and his sisters. Being a day-worker meant she would complete her employer's domestic chores in one day, chores which would otherwise be spread out over the period of a week. It was hard going but allowed her the opportunity to maximize her gross income. A day's work was paid an assigned rate and each employee was paid accordingly. At the end of the week her daily earnings accumulated to more than the weekly minimum wage for domestic workers. Sandra was determined to provide for her five children but Sheldon believed the food was never enough for the family and so pretended each day that he had eaten elsewhere just to make sure his sisters and mother had enough.

Sandra was acutely aware of her son's sacrifice and begged us to encourage him to eat the food she provided. When she saw no difference in his eating habits, she resorted to paying us for the weekly lunches sold at the canteen. She was a proud woman who did not believe in hand outs. Our organization placed the money in our welfare fund used to defray the costs of students like Sheldon who demonstrated the zealous determination to succeed but could not afford school fees to pursue a vocational training program. Despite his challenges, the teachers were confident Sheldon would achieve the required scores to be accepted in the national skills training program.

We had first met Sheldon two years before when he applied to the Grass Roots College, our Second Chance education program for school dropouts. An assessment showed that he was functionally illiterate. He could hardly write his name. Like many inner-city youth, Sheldon was frequently absent from the traditional high school that he attended because he did not have bus fare or lunch money and sometimes had no shoes. From the onset, the teachers observed Sheldon's quest for knowledge, his willingness to learn and his support to his peers. He would often stay after school to complete his homework assignment and it soon became a norm to see Fabian Bernard, 'Sir', the male teacher and school coordinator, helping him. Sir had taken him under his wing and mentored him. As anticipated, after two years Sheldon achieved the desired grades and graduated. It was expected that come September, he would attend the National Training Agency to pursue a career in carpentry. He declared, "The first house I am building is for my mother."

That August in 2005, true to his character Sheldon walked the streets of Kingston searching for a summer job. One day as we were leaving the office we saw Sheldon. He was running towards us grinning from ear to ear. He was sweaty and his shirt clung to his meagre frame. His shoes had taken a beating and his toes protruded through the sides. He excitedly waved a white piece of paper in front of us as he tried to speak slowly, "Sir! Miss Anje! Me get a jab, but di lady want you to call her first to recommend me."

We let out a cheer! Together, Sheldon, his teacher Miss Rose, Sir and I hugged and forming a circle; we danced and jumped, all the time shouting, "Yeah yeah yeah!" Everyone sprang into action. A letter of recommendation was written, and money was given to Sheldon to buy himself shoes and some new clothes for work. He promised to repay us when he received his first pay. We countered, suggesting that he repay us after he had built his first house. He grinned some more and was off.

Sheldon got the job. However, he soon called to say his employer was complaining that he arrived at work sweaty even early in the morning. She was impressed that he was always punctual but stressed the importance of presentation and recommended that he take the bus to work rather than walk. The problem was, Sheldon had no bus fare. So I had promised to meet him early to give him the day's bus fare, and enough for the remaining week. Only I was late.

I sped as fast as the traffic would allow thinking that I would make it up to him by taking him to work. Zzz, zzzz, the phone rang again, the ring-tone by Tony Rebel a persistent question, "If Jah is standing by your side... then.." I let the ring tone finish, thinking "I cannot be distracted by the phone... not now... Sheldon is waiting. I do not want to cause him to be late for work." The phone rang again. This time I picked it up. The background was noisy and I could hardly recognize the voice of Careen, our administrator. She was shouting, "Miss Stulllllz Miss Stulllz, where are youuuuu? Don't cooome." I didn't understand her. "What do you mean don't come, I am here." The phone went dead. It didn't matter. I was turning down St. Joseph Road where the clinic was located.

People were running down the street toward the clinic. From every yard at the top of the road, on both sides, the gates were flung open and people were running, everyone running in the same direction. Some were buttoning their blouses and shirts as if they were in the middle of getting dressed. The dogs were running beside them and barking excitedly. I was forced to stop driving as the large crowd in the street made it impossible for me to drive any further. I was now gripped with trepidation. I didn't know why, but I was feeling sick to my stomach. I got out of the car and joined the runners. Through the sea of faces I saw Sir, I saw other staff members, I saw their anguished faces, bodies bent over screaming, crying. Suddenly, I felt people's hands grabbing me, holding me back. It was too late. I saw Sandra on the ground, a body in her arms. She was telling him to get up. I saw the body. I saw Sheldon lying dead in a pool of blood.

Sheldon was killed while waiting for me. I had told him to wait. Don't leave I had said. In a flash, I broke free from the hands grabbing me and was on the ground with Sandra. It took many strong arms to lift us both up and away from the body. They could not console me, us. We were inconsolable. An innocent youth gunned down because of his affiliation to the section of the community where he lived. How could this be? How, how? Sheldon was known by everyone in the community. He was the proverbial choir boy, never involved in anti-social activity. The gangs on his side of the border had given up on him; Sheldon could not be recruited to even provide lookout service for them, so they ignored him. He had earned their respect and no one bothered him. As such, Sheldon freely walked throughout the community's lanes and borders at any time. But not that morning. Sheldon was waiting for me and became a victim of circumstance. With different sides of the community at war, a rival gang murdered him even though they knew he was not involved. The motive: a reprisal killing and a competition by the "hotheads" for the award of being the coldest.

Reprisal killings have no predictable rhythm or reason. Reprisal killings are influenced by a long history of feud, conflict and war between rival gangs. Hatred of each other is learnt and nurtured from their shared experiences of sporadic acts of revenge. In discussions with perpetrators they share similar stories of death caused by the other side. Each vehemently blames the other. Children from both sides of the invisible border live these experiences, and especially male children are fed the diet of hate seasoned with revenge. There is no healing, no restorative justice and they anxiously await growing up, ready to get even, to hurt the other side and hurt 'them' even more than they have hurt 'us'. Empirical data show that both the victims and the perpetrators of the nation's high homicide rate are male. Reprisal killings, as I have come to learn, are arguably parallel to racial and religious crimes. Nothing personal. It's just the 'Them' and the 'Us'.

I watched like an onlooker as my years of training in social work and psychology, of exercising emotional intelligence toward clients, went through the door. Years of upholding a professional image followed behind, and the years of guiding our organization by a fundamental non-biased principle followed in hot pursuit. I did not care. We had gone through many stages to gain the trust we now enjoyed from the community, and to be able to provide multi-faceted interventions with their buy-in and ownership. I knew we were treading on dangerous ground—my crying on the ground, the staff's public display of grief on the street—we had crossed the line. We understood the complexity of our actions. Crying for a youth who had died by external causes such as an accident or the police, drew unspoken understanding because it was neutral. Crying for a youth who was killed by another youth as we did exposed us, the organization, to a culture of speculation and interpretation. Our actions could confuse those we served and lead to a misconstrued perception of our alignment to one section of the community over another. Yet training and emotions refused to meet.

I tried to block the images of Sheldon waiting on me. I lamented that I should have told him to leave, borrow the bus fare from someone and I would repay. I blamed myself for telling him to stay. The self-blame held me captive and I prayed for release to cross the bridge of forgiveness. I was unable to. I felt the pain of a mother who had lost her son. In that moment I wholeheartedly embraced the culture of revenge.

The next day I feigned sickness to my children. I really wasn't pretending. I was physically, mentally and emotionally drained. I sent a message to the board of directors to manage the organization in my absence. They supported my decision. They informed me they had closed the school indefinitely; the students were traumatized and "Sir" had not shown up for class. The clinic's staff stopped working in demonstration of their outrage at the killing. I turned off my phone, instructed my children to say I was not home if anyone called and curled up in bed. And there I stayed, for three days.

My retreat was interrupted on the fourth day by a loud banging on the door. The banging was persistent and the caller refused to leave. It was my girlfriend, Carol. My other friends, Myrna and Lorna were globe-trotting and I had not spoken to them in the three days I was home. I knew they were worried about me but I did not feel like talking to them anymore. Their soothing voices made me cry harder. Try as I could, I could not stop crying. Moreover, I knew if Myrna were fully aware of my condition, she would drop everything she was doing and be on the first airplane back; a trip I knew she could not afford. Of the three friends, she was my 'ride and die chick', and earlier in the year had returned to care for me after a surgery I had undergone. Now I just wanted to be alone to wallow in my misery.

Carol Narcisse, who also served as a member of our organization's board, had heard of Sheldon's murder. We had enjoyed a friendship of over twenty years, sharing the same passion for community transformation. Carol was my reality check. She was gentle, yet assertive and extremely logical in her approach to life. I knew she would not leave until I opened the door. I let her in. She strutted past me, clicked on the lights and hugged me as a mother does with her child.

Carol listened attentively to me as I unloaded my state of mind through sips of mint tea she had made. She was a sharp listener, probing without judgment and possessed with the mind of a journalist. I let it all out: my intention to resign, my lost hope, feelings of revenge; I wanted a bulldozer to go and bulldoze the section of the community where the gang member who killed Sheldon lived. We could rebuild, I reasoned, providing examples of communities that were regenerated through new infrastructure and social interventions. She listened to my rambling, nodding, stopping me only for clarity about my ideas. And then she said. "Ok, I have arranged for all the staff to go on a week's retreat with a psychologist there to do group sessions but also one-on-one counselling. He is Dr. Geoffrey Walcott. He is very good and will be accompanied by Patricia Donald, a skillful facilitator, who will take you through therapeutic sessions. Don't worry about the cost, our funders/partners Jamaican Self-Help Canada and Christian Aid UK, have kindly provided support to cover the cost." That was Carol: holding her own emotions in check, taking charge, going the extra mile to make life better for her brood and others. Wise beyond her years.

The counselling sessions opened the gateway for a river of tears, honest self-evaluation and investigation of our faith. We had all taken Sheldon's death personally, not only because he was a student at the Grass Roots College, but each person and department had come to know him and about him because of his exemplary ambition. The canteen staff, clinic and project department, we had all been touched by his dreams, his care for his mother, his family, his resistance to the gang culture, and his determination to accomplish self-actualization. The impact of his death and the circumstances surrounding the incident challenged all we held dear. We looked at the poster displayed on the wall and read it with new eyes: When I grow up I want to be... ALIVE. We questioned how many youth we could mentor and channel in the direction of exemplary citizenry and then lose them to the very culture and situation we fought to keep them from. How many could we save, to grow up... alive? Our belief in social development theories and trust in God's intervention were severely tested.

The counselling sessions for staff allowed us the privacy and freedom to vent, blame, and express loathing of the oppressive system and perpetrators. We were reminded of the stories we had listened to, the tears of mothers, of parents, who sobbed for their dead child, asking us why. In response, we had offered counselling, referrals for further help, and pastoral and psychological care when the situation was beyond our capacity. Counselling was the primary prescription we gave for the many heartbreaking stories of striving young men who had lost their lives to gang violence. So many Sheldons.

The recommendations for counselling now seemed mechanical, empty. What did we know? How could we heal? We reviewed the primary reason for our organization's existence and mission, and examined who we were, our chosen career and our role. It was a painful and difficult process for us to fully reach acceptance and forgiveness in order to heal. It was especially hard for Sir and I. Sir had played a fundamental role in mentoring Sheldon and encouraging his dreams. And I had taken him under my wing, and it was me who he was waiting for on that fateful morning. I held on to Jehovah for healing and to forgive me. Slowly, very slowly we were brought back to focus.

From our own counselling we next extended grief counselling to the community. Kai Morgan a well-known counselling psychologist facilitated the first set of sessions with the women of the community. The first gathering was packed with women whose sons or family members had contributed to the high level of homicide victims in the national statistics. The participants also included a minority of women who had lost family members to natural causes. At first, the women did not mix with each other; they folded their hands across their bosoms and sat within their own groups. Some of them were angry, and their body language openly expressed their purpose in attending - to confront the women whose sons they held responsible for their hurt. Some were hurting so badly they were unable to cope with their grief and they did nothing but cry. The counsellor knew only too well the dynamics within the room and with great skill created a safe space for all.

A few months later Eva Dittrich, an American graduate student pursuing a degree in international service at the time, contacted me in Kingston seeking my help as a conduit to our community for her dissertation on the use of creative therapies in developing countries. After thoroughly vetting her and educating her about our neighborhood dynamics and safety risks, I arranged for her to meet with a group of women from the community who had all lost children to gang violence, whether caught in the crossfire or directly involved. Over the course of a few months, she gained the trust of the women, conducted personal interviews structured by the mothers, and held group meetings at the clinic. She provided individual cameras to the women and taught them how to use them with instructions to photograph important people, places, and things in their lives, including memories of their lost children. She provided photo albums and debriefing. Upon learning that several in the group had never been able to visit their children's graves due to distance and transportation cost, Eva contacted her favorite local cab driver, a Rastafarian nicknamed "Sam Cooke" for his singing voice, and the only driver she could convince to drive her to the bottom of St. Joseph Road where our clinic was. She arranged for him to take them on a day trip, allowing plenty of time and space at the cemeteries. The women were able to build a collage with pictures of the deceased, and places and events reminding them of their loved ones. Over the course of the project, the mothers were able to express themselves freely and grieve in their own personal ways, share and process their experiences safely, and learn to trust and support each other more. They shared in free-flowing discussions and had space to vent and roll on the floor if they wished to.

Both sets of counselling sessions provided the women with a greater sense of self-understanding and pride in having completed such a project. They also had created a support group which helped to reduce their avoidance of their traumatic memories, and strengthened them in their commemoration of their deceased children and their lives overall.

At the end of the program, women who began as arch enemies hugged, mingled and cried together, each feeling another's pain. The process of forgiveness and developing coping mechanisms had begun. Each woman was now responsible to help other family members to heal, particularly male family members. They would share the power of forgiveness to try to stem the reprisal killings and gang feuds and build better relationships.

In contrast to the impact on women of the community, our door to door mobilization for affected males to attend sessions did not yield the desired results. Not one male attended more than a single weekly session.

Occasionally, the group would be surprised by a male drop-in, but he would fidget and leave at the first opportunity. Jamaica is a patriarchal society and males are not socialized to cry or grieve in public. Instead, they carry around unresolved pain and anger which often results in physical attacks on loved ones or revenge on those they believe have caused them pain.

We resumed the organization's operation with the acute understanding that social practitioners also require counselling; that we are only human, social change agents, trying to be like Christ as we carry out a deliberately chosen career to change lives through the power of God. We understood the pain experienced by many mothers who have lost their sons through senseless killing, and it was for those very reasons that our organization existed. The experience humbled us and we learnt forgiveness, enabling us to reach grieving families in a more meaningful way. Our grief reinforced our commitment to continue our interventions, to advocate for change and facilitate empowerment for the vulnerable. Thankfully our organization's name and capacity to reach all its stakeholders were not affected by our visible, emotional breakdown and temporary closure. Overall, the community, including the perpetrators, understood.

As social workers we are trained to manage our emotions, to practice objectivity in order to conduct our work in a logical, non-discriminatory way. This is an important principle to practice in conflict mediation and especially in communities that are torn apart. But I am grateful for the empathy, passion and spirituality that allowed me to also cry, with the people with whom I have worked. I am grateful for the board of directors' understanding of staff needs to arrange counselling that helped us to revisit the organization's purpose. I am grateful that the community also received counselling and for us all to have an opportunity to rebound with deepened understanding and resolve.

Eva's Dittrich's story of S-Corner's impact on her life

My time in Kingston, Jamaica with Angela and the Waltham Park/Bennet land community women dramatically altered the course of my life, and I will forever be grateful for their trust in me. Their stories are burned into my heart and my memory, poignant as though they were relayed to me just yesterday. I carry them with me always.

All those who participated in my project lost children to gang violence, but they were so different, their coping reactions as unique as the women themselves. The individual interviews, part of the bigger project of mine that Angie described, lasted from thirty minutes to three hours and were mostly dictated by the participant. I was interested in as much as they wanted to share with me. They talked about their children and, when I asked about their life experiences, several remarked that no one had ever asked them. Beaming, proud smiles and giggles from one who told me she was pregnant, before she told the baby father, temporarily avoiding talking about a child she lost to crossfire. Another, barely surviving on beer and with tears silently streaming, described her desperation trying to find a doctor who would treat her child with cancer without the funds to pay, and just two years later finding her son shot to death in the street. She refused my lunch I tried to push on her every time we met, not out of contempt, but because she simply had no appetite...too much trauma. There was the woman who walked the long way to avoid *that* corner with *that* phone booth where her son was gunned down, and another who had to identify her son's shot, beheaded, dismembered body and then pretend she did not know his murderer as she passed him at the market several times a week. At only 16, he had made the fatal mistake of sneaking to an adjacent street to see a girl he liked and was fatally brutalized because of the deep hate of that gang towards the section he lived.

I'll never forget Angela's advising that I should conduct my individual interviews on the second floor of the S-Corner Clinic to limit my risk of getting caught in the crossfire during gang shootouts at the "Corner of Death," right outside the front door. She held everyone's stories too, here on St. Joseph Road much deeper than I, for years daily enthusiastically putting herself in harm's way physically and psychologically with the sole purpose of helping the residents. She is the keeper of the flame, a golden hero who deserves the notoriety that so many celebrities are given without warrant.

I have carried significant regret for the last thirteen years that, as a young graduate student on my own, I did not have the training or resources at the time to do more for these women, and I have always wanted to return to them. They need and deserve so much. I am so moved to know from Angela that my project helped them to heal in ways I hoped for but wasn't sure I was able to provide, that they felt seen and heard by me, and that they treasure their photo albums to this day. This project—these women—changed the course of my career; I thought I wanted to work solely as a humanitarian in community aid and development, but learned through my time in Kingston that mental health must be included in interventions for any programs to be truly effective. For example, microloans to individuals for small businesses are great, but if a person is traumatized, depressed, and can't eat or sleep, how far can it go? Money and practical aid is obviously necessary but not the entire answer. Psychological wellbeing is the foundation of everything in our world and needs to be treated as such everywhere, for both the privileged and underprivileged, the latter of whom are often forgotten or, worse, never seen in the first place. I also realized the crucial foundation of effective life coaching and psychotherapy long before I entered these fields: Asking people about their lives, thoughts, and feelings and listening with genuine interest makes them feel valued, many never get that, and everyone deserves it. You just don't know how far a little effort and kindness can carry someone, and even better if you can make real improvements with the right professional skills and resources.

Thanks to Angie's follow-up about my project, I have finally been able to let go a little of my regret that I could not fulfill the full needs of the ladies of St. Joseph Road and the Bennet land community, and am moving on to transforming my remaining heaviness into further helping action.

After Kingston, I continued on to finish my graduate program in International Service but then pursued more of an individual, intimate approach, completing my Life Coaching certification, studying Trauma and Violence Studies at NYU, and now finishing my Doctorate in Clinical Psychology at Pepperdine University. My passion for capturing the stories of individual women living in extreme poverty and helping them however I can, has carried into my doctoral dissertation and nonprofit organization called Shobha. Shobha seeks to help women with breast cancer living homeless in Los Angeles with a multidimensional, customized approach, something I call personal advocacy coaching.

I know that the women of St. Joseph Road have no idea how much our work together taught me and how they inspired me to help others, and I pray that one day I'll get to tell them how their bravery of being willing to actively participate in my project has carried on to touch the lives of so many others.

Eva Dittrich – 2006 "student"

Contact: Eva@EvaDittrich.com
www.EvaDittrich.com
www.ShobhaNetwork.org

SHINE AND SHUN

Shine and Shun

She walked with her head bent to the ground, shoulders hunched over, appearing to be looking for something lost and so small it required her intent gaze. Occasionally she kicked at orange juice boxes and plastic bottles as if they somehow blocked her path. The knapsack on her back protruded outward, forcing her to hunch over even further. In the opposite direction, Ms. Peggy passed her by and the child looked up to mumble something. We noticed she acted the same way with all adults who passed her, but our distance away made it impossible to hear. We speculated it was the customary greetings, recognition of a presence sharing the same space for a brief moment in time.

The acknowledgment is cultural, and an important indicator of respect especially for children in social interaction with their elders. Many Jamaicans have publicly expressed the concern that the culture of acknowledging persons is a dying practice especially in urban communities. The practice, or lack of it, is viewed as an outcome of good or bad parenting. The residents reason, "Pickney must have manners, they must say good morning, good evening, please and thank you to everybaddy. Mannas carry you a long way through the world."

We watched her from the top floor of the office. Her demeanor contrasted with the happy child prancing recently in our office. Only two weeks before Sade and her mother Miss Patta had stopped at the office to show off her uniform on her first day at a new school. Sade, a wide-eyed dark skinned child, rushed in ahead of her mother, threw her school bag on the nearest chair and did a 360 degree twirl for us. She continued her twirl, bouncing into staff members and prompting her mother's command for her to stop and be still. "Alright now Sade, stop, we see the uniform," she said. Sade, like all of us in the room, knew the request was not serious, just a contained effort from her mother to mask her own feelings of pride and joy and to impress us with her parental skill to restrain an overly excited child. Sensing that, the usually obedient child twirled and twirled again in a happy dance. Their excitement was contagious, and laughing, a staff member grabbed Sade as she twirled within reach.

It was the first day of class for Sade, at a new school many children envied and aspired to attend. Teachers worked assiduously to enable their students to achieve the required 100% grade average for acceptance in such a school. Based on the Ministry of Education's classification, this school was in the Tier 2 category nationally. It was a dream come true for any student to earn a place there, and Sade was the first child of the community to break that glass ceiling.

The majority of our Kingston 13 children attend one of three primary schools located within the geographic area. At age 12, the children transition to the two community-based high schools. These high schools are in the lowest assigned rank of the ministry. The local primary and high schools are generally overpopulated with an average of forty children squeezed in what looks to be little more than a ten-foot by ten-foot classroom. The schools are ill equipped - one black chalk board nailed to the wall and a teacher using a chalk to highlight main points of instruction. Being mindful that the students at the back of the room are unable to hear, the teachers shout across the room. Many of the students do not have breakfast and anxiously await the bell signaling the lunch break and the State-provided milk and sweet cake known as a "bulla". The children are no strangers to trauma. Academic reports confirm the startling data we already know: almost every single child has lost someone to violence, has witnessed domestic or gang related violence, and is affected by violence. Many children are sleep deprived because the street they live on is a war zone of rival gangs. For many, the classroom is a safe haven for sleep.

When the news came that Sade had gained a scholarship to attend a prestigious Tier 2 high school there was instant jubilation in the community's streets. Residents knew the significance. They reasoned, "when you go to dem type of school you become either teacher, doctor or lawyer." The possibilities to fulfill dreams resonated with them, "yu can rise from the zinc fence and become smaddy and make all a we proud!" So when they heard Sade's news, community women jumped, screamed and danced with each other. Young girls gyrated in the streets, happy at any opportunity to display the latest dance moves, while some banged the lids of cooking pots in celebration. Young children not fully grasping the meaning of the celebration still blew loudly on "fi-fi", colored horns usually blown at Christmas time. Miss Patta jumped and danced all the while holding the daily newspaper above her head for everyone to see. Men grinned, thumped fists and gave Sade's father, Mr. Clevie the high five all day long. He beamed with pride and boasted of his fatherly no-nonsense approach. He boasted, "Sade have fe study and do har homework or else!" He left the sentence unfinished for emphasis. Sade giggled and accepted the praises bestowed on her. She shined. It was a proud day and we all shined.

The jubilation confirms the fundamental similarities between people who share hopes and aspirations for a better life for each generation. That has not changed since my childhood days which were spent in the community called Standpipe, one of the poor neighborhoods located in the otherwise middle class Liguanea area, the outer area of what was known as the Golden Triangle. The affluent homes there provided employment to the families in my neighborhood –

domestic workers, chauffeurs, and gardeners. The community also provided skilled services and master tradesmen: mechanic shops, barber shops, tailors, seamstresses as well as small grocery shops. The close proximity of the neighborhoods, albeit class divided, provided us exposure to another way of life and influenced many poor families to push their children to become achievers. They understood the value of education and apprenticeship programs and their children were expected to do better than their parents, to become 'somaddy'.

In Kingston 13, everyone took pride in Sade's achievement. It became impossible for the teachers to conduct the usual homework assistance classes as residents from all sections of the community came to applaud, congratulate and even to register their own children for the upcoming term.

The services at our organization, the S-Corner Clinic and Community Center, included an educational assistance program each afternoon called "HAPPY" (Homework Assistance Program for Youth); the acronym was coined by Brian Hanley, a former international volunteer. It offered a combination of trained teachers, connectedness among students, and an understanding of each student's unique situation and academic challenges. In addition, our organization provided a conducive space for children aged 10-12 to read, participate in debates, get help with their homework assignments, or focus on preparing for the GSAT, a national high school entrance exam. Community volunteers serve as cooks to provide nutritional snack to the children, using vegetables grown in the community. The HAPPY program helped to provide inner city students the opportunity to improve reading, critical thinking skills and numeracy skills. And by so doing it helped to level, if even just a little, the playing field on which they competed with children from the private preparatory schools that were far better equipped with the tools to support learning. A goal of the HAPPY program was to increase children's grade level passes so that they could access the traditional grammar schools located outside of their community. This was a route to improving their life prospects. We saw many successes in helping children to gain passes to schools outside the community. Sade's achievement took her one step further by gaining entrance to a Tier 2 school.

So the jubilation in the street was understood. Sade's enthusiastic twirling on the first day was also understood. But what of this now slouched, hunched look of defeat after only two weeks' attendance at her new school? The male teacher Mr. Bernard playfully blocked her path. "What's up, Sade", he asked. "Nutten, sir", she responded, "I am just going home." Sir did not move; his intent was to engage her further before using the guise to invite her in to see the new batch of students.

Seeing that he was not going to let her pass, Sade shared her story: "Sir, di children dem don't talk to me, when lunch time come I sit by myself. Yesterday a girl name Anita was laughing' at my shoes, because it bursting on one side. I need shoes, but a don't want to stress mama because she couldn't even buy mi books dem. And, they serve cook lunch and all the students eat with knife and fork. I don't know how to use it, so most time I don't buy cook lunch even though it cheaper."

It took only two weeks for our shining star to become consciously aware of the difference in class stratification. The cultural differences and the mannerisms of the mostly middle class and affluent children made her doubt her ability to fit into the school. Jamaica is a stratified society that is sharply divided by class, a legacy from slavery and colonialism. Had it not been for the introduction of the Common Entrance Examinations for Jamaican students in the 1950s, many Jamaicans from humble beginnings would not have achieved any kind of social mobility. This examination system enabled numerous deserving students from impoverished communities to attend the higher tier institutions that were fully equipped with the educational resources, equipment and tools for learning.

Nevertheless, decades later, schools categorized Tier 1 and to some extent Tier 2 are still predominantly attended by wealthy and middle class Jamaicans. Our shining star became acutely aware of the social class stratification. Even though all the students wore uniforms, Sade lacked the social graces, etiquette, and mannerisms of the elite to be able to mingle unnoticed.

Her inexpensive shoes, which after only two weeks showed signs of wear, were visible indicators of her social class and made her stand out like a sore thumb. She felt shunned.

Sade's experience provided our organization with a new perspective on the issues that affect children's adaptability and subsequent learning in a new environment. Through this experience, the HAPPY program staff learned that while we placed emphasis on developing each student's academic and critical thinking skills, the program had not taken into consideration students' ability to assimilate outside of their social class. The question was, how could we as an organization help build students' confidence to interact, and reinforce their knowledge of their deserved rights to be a part of these educational institutions? How could we work to reduce the alienation that affected their confidence and ability to perform in these new environments?

A Board Director and famous musician, Mutabaruka, responded to Sade's plight by purchasing shoes and additional uniforms for her. He would continue to provide for her until her graduation. Meanwhile Careen, our organization's Administrator, took Sade under her wing for life-skills and etiquette lessons. Our organization also encouraged Sade to continue reading books outside of school assignments to broader her horizons. Sade's outward appearance and skills contributed to her improved social interactions but she gained more from her avid reading which built her self-worth, confidence and sense of belonging.

Ultimately, self-worth and confidence come from within and should be nurtured by parents and school stakeholders. For grassroots organizations, we could focus on nurturing one child at a time, which would benefit the individual child and community. The HAPPY program was intended to fill a gap within the community by supplementing the efforts of existing elementary school programs so that more local children would be eligible for Tier 1 or 2 high schools. However to be sustainable, ultimately the change needs to be at a more systemic level with equity among all elementary and high schools.

Some years later, representatives of Jamaican Self-Help Canada, the financial partner that supported the HAPPY program, paid a visit to one of the community's elementary schools. They were conducting a monitoring and evaluation exercise. A young lady walked over and twirling in full circle, hugged one of the team members she recognized. That young woman is a teacher at the school, a graduate of the Mico Teachers College, boasting a first degree in Education. In addition to her lesson plans for the three Rs, this teacher adds social skills to her curriculum: she tutors her students in how to sit, to be fluent in English grammar and in how to carry themselves. She teaches them how to eat with a knife and fork. She goes the extra mile to build their confidence and self-esteem. That teacher's name is Sade.

FREEDOM FESTIVAL

Freedom Festival

Kites of assorted shapes, sizes, and colors filled the morning sky and soared above us. It was a windy day in June and the breeze took hold of them and propelled them further up before they took a nose-dive down, then up and up again, giving the impression to the onlookers below that they were now smaller. Long kite-tails trailed behind and they appeared to be dancing to the sounds of the wind, whuuf whuuiff. The kites climbed steadily upward forcing the excited onlookers below to crane their necks backwards to watch them as they soared to new heights. They soared across the open field, across the community boundaries, and into new territories. This was the Freedom Festival, a kite flying competition, where the kites above symbolized a new found freedom experienced by those who held their strings.

The kite owners, alleged gangsters, watched their kites with awe. Mesmerized. With careful and deliberate ease, they unwound and lengthened the strings to increase the kites' ability to go further. It was as if each kite represented the owner's yearning to experience real freedom, moving beyond the confined social and economic boundaries of the community without fear. For them, fear was a constant energy. Fear of rival peers, fear of the police and fear of society's scorn. The kite could be made to explore other spaces and places not yet seen, and more importantly helped the men experience the life of a free man, free from the burden of the gangster's life, always wanted, always blamed, the victim or the perpetrator. Either way, incarcerated in his turf.

The residents watched with fascination those holding onto the kites. They watched the grinning adolescents, proudly showing off their mastery in kite flying. These youth bore no resemblance to the dangerous and disreputable characters community members had come to know and the wider public imagine.

These now-happy adolescents were gang members and former gangsters who resided in and controlled opposing turf. By virtue of inherited feuds and allegiance to their turf, each one had his fair share of blame for the maiming, hurting and alleged killing of others who, in some instances, were innocent persons whose only crime was their residential location. The kite flyers had the infamous status of notorious gunmen; they were feared, revered and were hunted by law enforcement agents and rival gangsters alike. In a bid to live beyond the gangsters' average life span of twenty-five years, these youth protected their identity and were rarely if ever seen publicly. They were usually unable to participate in community events, let alone participate with their opponents.

But a new freedom resulted from a peace initiative brokered by the S-Corner Centre. Residents now enjoyed long forgotten privileges: passengers of taxis who would normally be let off at the top of the main road were now driven to the nearest point, greatly benefitting pregnant women, the elderly, and women returning from markets with heavily laden bags. Social gatherings had increased, segmented along gender-specific lines: females according to their age gathered in front of their yards, old men sat under trees playing dominoes, and male youths gathered on the corners. Community artisans, businesses and the community economy were revived and booming. Outsiders tentatively entered the community in search of the most skilled dressmakers and tradesmen, venturing down the narrow dirt lanes because of the obvious, multiple symbols of peace: noise rather than eerie silence, busy streets, children playing in the streets, dogs barking at passersby.

The kite flying day was symbolic of a new journey the youth had embarked on six months before, a journey which they had charted together to end the gang war between them. This was a journey that involved the seemingly impossible—rival gangsters having civil relationships, the first step towards community peace. The Freedom Festival, a kite flying competition, was an unprecedented event that brought together gangsters who had signed a Memorandum of Agreement to end the spate of reprisal killings. After weeks of joint labor to construct a sports area, designing and creating assorted kites, the day arrived when they would compete in sports. In day light. The rules of the game were to be observed by all; competitors and allies would wear only thin undershirts or nothing to cover their upper body, leaving nowhere to conceal a gun. The dress code would make them vulnerable but also would give them the unfamiliar approval they needed from the community and police. It brought a glimpse of freedom.

A police patrol car moved from one end of the road to the next at bumper-to-bumper traffic pace; the policemen nodding salute to residents as they passed. Their guns rested across their laps as they watched the cheering crowd and youth running across the field with brightly colored kites in hand. Residents waved to the police as they drove by. They surmised that even with their guns resting across their laps, the policemen appeared to have left their usual intimidating presence behind.

The Freedom Festival was new and the patrol cops, though wary and alert, were supportive. Their superiors had briefed them of the day's event, the profile of the competitors, and the day's objectives. The importance of their role as peace officers was stressed: to protect and enhance safety for all, through increased police patrols... just in case. The police presence further motivated the minority of cautious residents to come out of their homes and support the venture. Nevertheless, these residents kept to the outskirts of the street, ready to sprint at the first hint or possibility of conflict.

The community grapevine would later relate stories of residents who had stayed away, using alternative routes for commuting on the event day in order to avoid the open field and the immediate sections of the community adjoining the field. News of who the competitive teams were had provoked incredulous responses like that of Miss Thomas, "Me mam, what me doing near dem there yute? Suppose one of dem step on the other one toe. Lawd Jeesus, Miss Angie, the clinic people mad!" And who could blame those residents for their skepticism and fear of being close to youths who used guns and other weapons as their only means to settle their conflicts?

Community life had swung between peace and stability, and gang war and instability. Neither was a new phenomenon to the community. This would be our organization's third major effort at a peace intervention. Previous truces were broken by factors appearing trivial on the surface. Each time the community moaned in frustration and grief. As social change practitioners our experience contradicted arguments that the reasons were trivial. Gang wars are ugly symptoms of underlying root causes: systemic structures of inequality that deprive access to education, the means to a dignified life, and social mobility. Systems that provide privileges based on race and class. We have learnt that peace in community means the absence of gun shooting, while guns remain accessible. We have learnt where there is abject poverty, high illiteracy and high levels of underemployment, there will be fights for the control of scarce benefits.

The Freedom Festival was one of several crucial activities in this round of peace. In 2006, shootings and reprisal killings were again affecting our organization's social intervention programs and community stability. Student attendance at our educational programs dwindled to an all-time low as fearful parents kept their children inside. In contrast the clinic staff was bombarded with patients requiring dressing for new wounds. The situation worsened daily. The organization had to do "sumpting".

In one month a six-year-old girl was shot in the leg and five youth died, among them Nicole allegedly by a policeman's gun. Residents describe how Nicole, was walking along Crescent Road, at the same time the police alighted from a jeep, shooting at a group of youth they recognized as "wanted men". I have no words to describe her mother Annette's anguish, the total despair of her only female child's death, and the physical and psychological decline we witnessed. We held her, we organized support in a way that she would not feel overwhelmed and then alone; there was always someone with her, we encouraged her laughter and tears, and we prayed. The tension was further exacerbated when one morning the staff noticed the telltale sign of bullets having shattered the window panes of the north and south windows of our office.

Then came February 14, Valentine's Day. The female staff had worn white and red in recognition of the day. The morning's compliments and wishes of Happy Valentine's Day were cut short by the sound of gun shots at close range. In automatic Dive-Lie flat-Head down (DLH) response staff and patients scattered under tables and desks. White outfits absorbed the floor's red oak stains and were now different shades of brown and red. We resented being on the ground rolling and slithering like snakes in open grass. Valentine's Day is lovers' day after all! Earlier feelings of fear turned into anger and people grumbled loudly so everyone could hear, "Me cant bother wid dis work, look how me did look nice this morning and now me fayva dutty bus." This was accompanied by loud hissing of teeth, "We too old, too tired of this shit. We tiaad!!"

The Dons respected our organization for its long-standing work in the community, but more so because it was managed by a Rastafarian Empress who instilled in them the value of life. The occurrence of day-time shootings therefore signified that the violence had reached new heights and the need for revenge superseded the relationships we had. It was a turning point for the worse and it cried out for a critical evaluation of our program's impact, for proactive action —to quit or to do things differently.

Previous efforts at peace had included one in 1996 that was initiated by community women and the second in 1999 led by one of the gang leaders. Each time, the gang leaders had verbally pledged to settle potential disputes in amicable ways and maintain peace. Each peace lasted an average of two years.

Attorney at Law Sajoya Alcott listened attentively and without interruption to my concern for there to be lasting community stability, my frustrations with earlier peace efforts, and finally my request for her help to try something different. She was my legal advisor, my friend, my sistah and someone I trusted with my life. She was smart, beautiful, and one of the best criminal defense lawyers the country produced. She had given up her criminal practice at the height of her career to instead represent musicians and artists in their contractual agreements. She said something to the effect of, "Knowledge of the law and the lack of eyewitnesses enabled me to win a homicide case which kept me awake at nights. Defending the rights of artistes and musicians is more in keeping with my values. I can sleep now." She was key to the plan I had developed: to use lessons learned, build on our former efforts, and try one more time to create lasting peace.

Sajoya's relationship with well-known and internationally famous reggae artistes was the link needed to rally musicians for this peacemaking cause. Our first call was to Patrick Barret aka Tony Rebel who would provide invaluable service to mobilize other musicians and lead a committee. The committee members were singer Jepther McClymont - Luciano, DJ/singer; Ventrice Morgan - Queen Ifrica, DJ/singer; Italee Watson-Italee, dub poet; the late Sandra Alcot-Sajoya; and poets Neto Meeks and his Royal African Soldiers group. The committee members were mostly Rastafarians and were happy for the opportunity to engage and mentor young males. Mutabaruka, internationally known dub poet and already a board member for some ten years, also joined the committee. With that, the Committee for Community Peace (CCP) was born.

The CCP would call on the leadership of Mutabaruka and Tony Rebel to use their persuasive abilities to influence the other committee members to venture into the lanes to meet with the gang members, build relationships and begin the process of trust building. The musicians, like many faith-based or conscientious Jamaicans, wrestled with their moral desire to become actively involved in community upliftment and the involuntary trepidation they experienced upon entering the war torn, inner-city community. They were cognizant that a primary component of any peace keeping intervention was trust building, which meant intense engagement, weekly visits, and meetings held in different sections with rival gang members. For them it was also a huge career risk which they contemplated.

What about the police? Would they be sacrificing their reputation when word got out that they were meeting with hard-core criminals, alleged murderers? Moreover, where was the church in all this? According to one musician, "Sis Angie, we sing about peace because we believe positive message reinforce positive behavior, but we not social workers."

Our organization had learned valuable lessons from its previous peacemaking efforts. One such lesson was that ultimately peace building must be owned by the direct perpetrators, and the gang leaders had responsibility to confront and engage each other in discussion. The burning question of how to make this happen was the CCP's task. How to bring them in eye-to-eye contact without looking in the barrel of a gun? The CCP divided its members in three teams each charged with the same task – to get the buy-in of gang members for a face-to-face meeting. This meeting would be a private meeting between gangsters only and held outside of the community. Achieving this task was contingent on the teams' ability to win the trust of their assigned gang members. The proposed meeting would allow gangsters the opportunity to discuss the issues that encouraged gang conflict, ways of settling conflict, actions or events for possible unified, long term stability, and how to get mainstream civil society's support for their efforts to maintain a socially cohesive community.

Another important lesson of our previous efforts was the need to build relationships with the police, the

Jamaica Constabulary Force. The objective was to facilitate police buy-in to our transformation methodology by showing how it would enhance their community policing approach and rebuild a tattered relationship with residents. Relationship building with the police required a mechanism similar to the one we used with the underworld: systematic meetings with the senior superintendent of police and other high ranking officers in charge of the division. The meetings were led by the then new board chairperson, Carol Narcisse. It was no easy task.

Some high-ranking police objected. They argued that civil society would be safer if the alleged perpetrators were behind bars or eliminated. We countered that society would be better off if they were rehabilitated, giving examples of behavioral changes that showed peers and the future generation that alternative lifestyles were possible. The Senior Superintendent SSP Newton Amos, a veteran serving in the police force for over twenty years, argued on our organization's behalf that hardcore policing by itself was not sufficient for the desired outcome of reducing homicides. He was a tough cop, and at the same time a progressive critical thinker who saw the role of the JCF in constructively creating an environment of peace and safety for all citizens. His experience showed that police aggression was met with equal aggression from the youth. He welcomed new ideas that incorporated citizens' involvement and police integration in the community. For example, SSP Amos requested our CCP collaboration in one of his programs:

to influence the local sound system operators and dance hall promoters to desist from the practice of playing dancehall songs that incited and applauded violence at the community dancehall events. The CCP Committee agreed to partner on this venture and we had his blessing. We would update him on the days the musicians were in the community and the progress being made. We had his assurance that we need not fear he would send his troops in to cause any 'informa' branding or even more deadly, a shootout between police and gunmen.

The weekly line up of well-known personalities and prestigious motor cars driving through their inner-city community sparked residents' interest and excitement. The artistes were at first treated with all the fanfare that accompanied famous people. People asked them to spontaneously sing, perform at their next fundraiser or give them money for groceries. The artistes took it all in stride, and when they later dispersed as teams to facilitate meetings with their assigned gangs, the community took notice. Soon community residents quit begging and requesting spontaneous performances. The residents interpreted the weekly encounters to be more valuable than the chances to obtain individual, short-term gains. The shooting between rival gangs stopped and the community recuperated from its violent set-back. Community members and gangs too began to feel they mattered. Important people, civil society leaders and famous musicians were trekking through their dirt lanes, sometimes jumping over smelly sewage, sitting in their yards to talk sense to their children, sons and family members, and to offer condolences to those who were grieving. Ghetto lives actually mattered. Nevertheless, it would take the CCP two months of intense meetings before the gang leaders conceded to meet with each other. And this time on our organization's terms.

Our terms demanded trust, 'full thrus" as one leader summarized; the gangsters had to have total faith in the Committee. They had to trust us, trust that our relationship with the police did not mean betrayal of their confidentiality, that we were non-judgmental, non-partial and no information would be disclosed to their rivals, and they would not end up dead if they went with us. Last but certainly not least, they had to know that we would not become state witnesses against them based on the information they had shared.

The process meant we, every single member of the committee, musicians and staff, were also putting our lives at great risk. We were privy to information allowed only to priests. A single misinterpreted piece of information, a single perception of trust and confidentiality broken, and all gains would be lost, for both our organization and for us. We would all die. Our fate was that horribly simple.

The risks we were all taking in trust building was overwhelming but so too was the knowledge of its dire importance. Gun slaying and violence was an unacceptable, morally wrong way of solving conflict. Gangsters and the CCP proceeded to stage two: for them to accompany us to an unknown but safe venue outside of the community. Each group would identify their most influential and valuable leader, as well as their second in command; they would hand over their mobile phones to us, thus ensuring they could not make any phone calls, and surrender their guns to us for safe keeping. To maximize feelings of safety for everyone, we had to conduct body searches of the gangsters which they would allow to be done by females only. Through coincidence or perhaps divine intervention, each team included one female who carried out body searches requiring us to feel alongside intimate body parts. This the men did not mind!

Our organization booked a conference room in one of Kingston's four star hotels for the day, inclusive of three meals. The CCP had no idea how long the process would take for the gangsters to reach an amicable solution but the committee was prepared to spend the night if necessary. One by one the cars arrived at the venue and gang members alighted. The facial expressions were so similar and almost amusing to watch, though we dared not laugh. Every gang member appeared visibly shaken when he recognized the persons exiting the other cars. On reflex, some gangsters reached to pat their waists. There was nothing to feel. We had taken whatever they were feeling for, along with their phones, and these were labeled and stacked in safe places. One person went immediately in search of the bathroom—we were not sure if he went in search of anything that could be transformed into a weapon, or simply for a mentally induced calling.

A total of twenty-four persons sat around the conference room. Nine nervous committee members and fifteen suspicious gang members. The gangsters included a lone female. She was short and hefty and was known to gun-butt anyone who crossed her. A member of the CCP prayed for divine intervention. All eyes remained wide open and no one even bothered to hold their head down in reverence. We all felt the urgent need to call on the presence of God, the supreme Jehovah right there and then. The meeting was nerve wracking for all, more so when every gangster politely refused to eat the first meal placed in front of them, saying they were not hungry.

Sajoya facilitated the meeting and in her usual quiet but commanding tone she laid the groundwork for engagement: respect for each other and their patience to listen to each other. Predictably, the meeting began with gangsters blaming each other for the declined state of the community, the ongoing feuds and reprisal shootings. No one was owning their role or taking responsibility for their actions. Two hours into the discussion nothing had changed and CCP members frequently visited the bathrooms. A gang member boasted to another that, "One morning me have you in clear shot", but a woman had crossed the line of vision and he didn't bother to shoot him. A rival member from that gang pointed to another leader and gave a similar story of how close he had come to shooting him, but, "Same time me see you madda an never bodda". The stories of near misses, of times they had chased each other, of when one could have shot the other and didn't, were shared among them. Someone cracked a joke and slowly the mood changed. Bread was broken and we ate breakfast at about noon.

The following session explored the impact of reprisal killings and unearthed shifting emotions among the gangsters - both anger and empathy. At times, the pent-up anger spewed across the table, hung in the air and became so toxic the CCP had to pause the meeting to remind persons of the rules of engagement. Ninety per cent of the gang members had witnessed or shared similar pain of losing a "dawg" beside him, and all were equally guilty of causing each other the pain they endured. We spoke to them of rules made in the 1997 peace effort eighteen years before; that one of their deceased leaders said, "How can we swop a live man for a dead man." The discussion provided timelines of persons killed, how each gangster on both sides had embarked on a campaign of vengeance advocating an eye for an eye and giving rise to the homicide count and grief. They pointed fingers. "It was you do this that's why I did that." We silently thanked God there was no weapon in sight.

Suddenly, Kutu leaned forward across the table and raised his hands signaling he wished to speak. Calmly he said, "Well gentlemen, hear dis, Joe just say him line up a man cross the road and could a pick him off, so I know we have the same things dem. Anyone a we ya so could a be a victim. Cause no man no fear de next man. The thing is we can done it, or we can see who dead off first." The room became deadly silent as gangsters processed the information Kutu had just summarized. They were all equally equipped with the weapons of destruction to eliminate one another. The CCP watched as reprisal killings took on new meaning, and the gangsters looked at one another with a new lens of understanding and empathy. Without verbalizing the words, "I am sorry", each youth related a story of a time when someone on the opposite side had died and of the genuine pain he felt. At that point a well needed break was called.

The next session explored the lifestyles of a gangster, how the conflict impacted them and their community. The impact list was long and was injected with odd humor as the gangsters described intimate details of their lives: lack of sleep, no sex, no family life and church people praying for their demise. They explained how they would be up all night on the look out to ward off an ambush from rival gunmen, and during the day they were denied the luxury of even a nap due to the heavy police presence. They talked about their dysfunctional sex and family life, how church women dressed in red head ties would stop on their corner and spin around three times while screaming prophesy of their impending death. Earning from any hustling was out of the question, as they had to be in hiding. And much worse, the community and nation blamed them for the country's social ills and community degradation.

By nightfall, the gangs showed a deepened understanding of the pain they caused each other and by extension the community. This meeting was the first time in many years or ever that these youth who lived in the same neighborhood, with some of them attending the same primary schools, had spoken to each other. The conversation in a safe space, free from worrisome encounters with each other and the police allowed them to listen to each other. Additionally, the CCP facilitation and input in the discussion allowed the gangsters to examine their actions. With new insight they developed a code of conduct to be adhered to if there was to be lasting peace.

1. Mediation and communication: CCP members would be first response mediators for potential gang conflicts.

2. Phone numbers shared between leaders, to be used only to reduce conflicts not threats.

3. Leaders responsible to guide/discipline their members in actions for peace keeping.

4. Leaders responsible to communicate with other leaders if a member created conflict with the other.

5. No sexual harassment of females in rival sections to send messages and provoke conflict.

6. Fair distribution of political contracts and jobs when assigned to one group.

7. Joint income projects that would increase visibility of togetherness in community.

8. Sport competitions in friendly rivalry to promote community cohesion.

9. Systematic round robin dances held in all sections to increase movement and revolving income, each would support other sections.

The week following the meeting, all nine members of the Committee for the Community Peace (CCP) fell ill and were unable to carry out their functions. Each had extended him/herself to act on their beliefs, but in a way that was mentally, physically and spiritually draining. The meetings, and particularly the final face to face meeting of the gangsters, had encouraged honest discussions which allowed them to let go of pent-up anger and feelings of vengeance toward each other. The CCP members had absorbed it all. Yet despite our exhaustion, we were all gratified with the process' success, and grateful and humbled by the experience of Jehovah's divine intervention that guided and protected us throughout our work.

Three months after the meeting, the gang members joined resources to embark on two projects. The first was to construct a bamboo wall around an open unused lot of land to transform it into the sports area they now enjoyed for the Freedom Festival. This project entailed former rivals using sharp machetes, sometimes side by side, to de-bush and clear the land. Even more alarming to the faint of heart was the fact that rivals would drive off together to purchase various construction materials outside of their community. At first, the community's residents waited with heightened apprehension and speculated if these actions were a good thing. They speculated that one day only one would return and report that there had been an accident or something that took the other person's life. Gradually residents relaxed and allowed themselves to welcome the change that had happened.

Today the Freedom Kite Festival was on the open lot they had labored to create. The police presence and visible integration in the community, encouraged and cemented community cohesion and by nightfall doubtful residents came out and joined in the now festive community atmosphere. For the first time in many years, families across the divide openly mingled and without fear of returning home.

The other joint activity by the gang members was the staging of a musical fundraising event. The CCP members mobilized other famous musicians who performed voluntarily. On the night of the event, rain fell heavily but could not damper the mood of residents and patrons who danced all night to reggae music and clean dance hall lyrics. The musical event attracted media attention and was a huge success, in both community involvement and financial returns. The proceeds were divided equally among the three major gangs, each embarking on an income generation program of their choice. The resulting businesses were bag juice making, chicken rearing, and pig rearing. The gangs' involvement in income generation, the musicians' roles as mediators, organized programs and exposure beyond the immediate community, were all integral to cementing relationships between the formerly warring factions, and supporting community peace.

Youth Interactive, an NGO operating in Santa Barbara responded to our organization's proposal to decentralize our Youth Empowerment Program. The program involved the construction of a computer center in the most densely populated section of the community, so as to maximize reach to our targeted population. The building construction created yet another opportunity for former rival gangs to jointly provide sweat equity for the community betterment. The Youth Empowerment Program further provided the resources for community youth to use information technology and to connect with other youth across the globe sharing knowledge and culture. The youth center was also used for for organized homework, community meetings, youth club, and women support meetings. The youth center soon became the hub of that section, with the youth adding a barber shop for income generation.

This time, community stability/peace lasted for well over seven years and was broken only by the death of the main leaders. There was much to learn from this outcome and why it was achieved.

- The process had benefitted from all the earlier peace processes—it didn't happen in a vacuum.

- Residents of inner-city communities are not different from other people in their desire for respect. They discern and are responsive to being treated with respect and as an equal.

- The willingness of the police, SSP in charge of local police station to collaborate with civil society groups.

- Patient listening pays. Having facilitators who listen more than they speak assures those who share that they and their stories matter

- Trust is the most valuable asset.

- Our organization's multifaceted programs reached all community members and had gained respect and trust from diverse stakeholders, including the police force, civil society groups, gang members and community residents themselves.

S-Corner Clinic & Community Development Organization was an oasis in the desert, a beacon of hope to the residents, and an organization living up to its mandate to facilitate change in people's lives and the stigma attached to their community address. The impact of our interventions transcended to the national level, helping to reduce the statistics for homicide and violence, unemployment and the burden on health care, and providing second chance education to drop outs.

There is much to be done to reclaim our community and country. The hope of *Signs and Wonders: Sojourn in the Inner-city* is to inspire Jamaicans in the diaspora, non-government organizations, private sector agencies, churches, and international partners to continue to advocate for policy changes at the macro level, hold our successive governments accountable to serve our people with integrity and provide the necessary financial and material resources to make communities and Jamaica the paradise we know it can be.

EPILOGUE

Epilogue

My work in the inner cities of Jamaica, Kingston, Spanish Town, Maypen and Montego Bay span over twenty years. I believe I have fulfilled some of my life's purpose that I was created to do. It's been a journey that called upon my Faith in God, Jehovah as I refer to the Highest Creator of the Universe, and the study of social science with emphasis on youth and community development. Both faith and social work commitments were tested and created conflict and self-doubt within me, my values, as well as tensions that arise between the responsibilities to guide persons into rehabilitation without obstructing the laws of the land.

Since 1992, I have led/managed two well-known NGOs in developing and implementing diverse educational, social, psychological, health and sanitation, infrastructural and economic intervention programs in inner-city neighborhoods. These two NGOs, S-Corner Clinic & Community Development Organization and the Rose Town Foundation for the Built Environment, are located in Kingston's inner-city communities,

Waltham/Bennetland and Rose Town. Like many other inner-city neighborhoods, they are characterized by high unemployment, underemployability among youth, teenage pregnancy, poor sanitation and gang violence. There is much to be done to eliminate multigenerational poverty by addressing the underlying causes. The political will and investment of capital are needed to level the playing field. The inequalities and disparities between the haves and have-nots are glaring. Just take a fifteen minutes ride to or from New Kingston and the question is likely to arise: Is this the same Jamaica, and more so, Kingston?

With creativity, commitment, resilience and the Power of the Most High God, we have achieved tangible successes, and in the process have changed lives and conditions.

At the time of writing I had many chance meetings which I interpret as other Signs and Wonders to be mentioned in this book. I met Mark Fisher at the Half Way tree bus station who now supervises a fleet of Jamaica Urban Transit Company (JUTC) buses and who reminded me of who he was in order to say thank you.
I met "Criminal" in New Kingston who has changed his name and life direction. He is now gainfully employed and a God-fearing man living with his wife and family and who said "Miss Angie, S-Corner save me but a can't even look back down there". I ran into "Barry" for whom Carol Narcisse and I purchased the plumbing tools he needed so that he could escape the gang life and

start anew. He now resides in rural Jamaica and is an established plumber. Rosalee Mcbean, who found me on Facebook. She is a 1998 Grass Roots College graduate, who went on to complete the Practical Nursing course, now an OB Technician working in a Chicago hospital. Rosalee called to say, "Thank you Miss Angie, I never got the chance to tell Marlene (now deceased) "Thanks" but I want you to know, S-Corner Grass Roots College made me the success I am today."

Signs and Wonders captures my relationship with God and how he manifests himself within me and to me as I carry out development work in the inner-city. It has been a truly gratifying experience.

I would like to sum up my work with a quote by an unknown author.

Jah looked down at my work and Smiled

And then he looked again and saw my salary

He Cried.

And so he provided, so much I am able to give freely without expectations. Thank you, Jehovah for your mercies and blessings for the Signs and Wonders throughout my journey.